NEW FOREST
• PONIES •

NEW FOREST
·PONIES·

architects of the Forest

DIONIS MACNAIR

Whittet Books

Frontispiece: stallions off the Forest running together in New Park, autumn 1904.

First published 2006
Text © 2006 by Dionis Macnair
Whittet Books Ltd, Hill Farm, Stonham Road, Stowmarket, Suffolk
IP14 4RQ

British Library Cataloguing in Publication Data
A catalogue record for this book is available from the British Library

ISBN 1 873580 69 X

The author and publishers are grateful to the following for permission to use photographs on the pages listed: Mrs Helen Beale p 23; Linda Charles p 2, p 20, p 22, p 24, p 68, p 112, p 165 ; Property of NFPPG/ Sally Fear p 29; Robin Fletcher p 42; Forest Reflections p 4, p 15; Mark Freeman p 121; New Forest Photographs 16; Pleasure Prints p 66; Anthony Reynolds p 83, p165; Still Images p 115; Barry Whitcher p 13, p 29, p 64

Otherwise photographs are the property of the New Forest Pony Society or the New Forest Pony Publicity Group and we are grateful for their permission to reproduce.

Printed and bound by Cromwell Press Trowbridge

CONTENTS

1
EARLY DAYS

RIGHT IN THE MIDDLE OF THE SOUTH OF ENGLAND, between the rapidly growing conurbations of Bournemouth and Southampton, is what has been described as 'a little piece of mediaeval England'. Behind the mainly urbanized coast is an area of heathland, acid grassland, bog, more prettily now called mire, and ancient pasture woodland. This is the ancestral home of the New Forest pony. The open Forest, together with the timber growing enclosures, is administered by the Forestry Commission for the Crown, as the Forest is part of the Crown lands handed over at the start of each reign in exchange for the civil list. The villages, with their small pasture fields, in and around the Crown lands, are privately owned and are where the Commoners who own the ponies live.

It used to be thought that the Celts introduced the ponies but it is now considered probable they were here much earlier, soon after the last ice age and that, with wild cattle and deer, they and the Forest evolved together, and are interdependent. Herds of ponies ranged right across Britain. Bronze Age farmers cut down some of the forest to make fields to grow corn but the soil was thin and without the trees soon leached away, just as is happening in the rain forests today. Here the result was heath and impoverished pasture. The resulting moor and bog was abandoned by the farmers leaving the pony herds cut off from each other. When these ponies passed into private ownership is lost in the mists of time but it probably happened gradually, some domestic horses would have escaped and bred while some of the wild ones were caught and tamed. Mares caught would be branded and their future foals considered the property of the owner of the brand. Hamlets remained in the more fertile valleys except where a plug of impervious clay had formed a dam and here the result was bog. The streams normally overflow in very wet weather but hopefully flow back quickly leaving a fertile sediment behind so the stream side lawns are the best grazing.

The earliest representation of a New Forest pony is an unflattering child-like decoration on a pot fired at Linwood about 300AD. Of about the same date part of the skeleton of a pony standing about 12.3hh has been excavated at the Roman Villa at Rockford. Canute's Forest Law 1016 mentions ponies among the wild animals of the Forest.

During the Middle Ages there was a Royal Stud in the Forest to which, in 1220, eighteen mares from Wales were sent. In 1217 Henry III ordered the profit for the year from this stud to be given towards the building of Beaulieu Abbey. Manwood's Law of the Forest quotes Henry VIII ordering the removal from all Royal Forests of 'stoned horses of less than 14 and a half handfulls'(stallions not exceeding 14.2 hh) and the slaughter of mares unsuitable for breeding. Manwood regretted this law was no longer in force. It is probable it never was enforced, he was writing 200 years later. Local people would have known the smaller ponies thrived better and in any case the ponies still had to be caught. The later Deer Removal Act luckily failed to remove all the deer. However, as this was long before the better land was enclosed for timber growing, it would have supported a rather bigger pony and Continental horses, mainly from Spain and the Low Countries, are known to have been imported to improve local stock in Tudor times. These imports probably introduced the colour chestnut and white markings into the breed. Elizabeth, daughter of James I, is reputed to have had a Forest pony.

On June 13th, 1517, Lord Thomas Howard reported that two ships had sailed for the war in France with 'Many small men, some with the King's mounts of the New Forest.' If this was just part of the baggage train he would not have mentioned it. The chances are that 'small' relates to the men's social status, not their height, i.e. they were small Commoners but unlike small holders in the rest of the country who would have had nothing to do with horses, small Commoners would be experienced horsemen and so good cavalry men. Henry was trying to raise the height and quality of horseflesh by passing the act prohibiting the use of 'stoned horses of less than 14 handfulls'.

The knight in armour on his great horse had been made redundant by gunpowder and the army required a lighter more athletic animal. These were bred in Spain where the Moors had introduced Arab blood and crossed it with native mares to breed the ancestors of the Andalucian and Lippitzana horses. These quickly spread all across the Spanish Empire, notably to Vienna and the Low Countries. Since they were the type of horse that everyone who could afford them wanted, trade brought them to England. Every native breed has the myth of the stallion that swam ashore from the Armada – certainly not possible in the Forest; there were no wrecks on the South Coast. As we know

Gilpin's etching.

there was a Royal Stud in the Forest it seems very probable Spanish stallions stood there and were crossed with the local ponies to breed these more athletic mounts. This would be the first chance to try them in action. We also have stories of veteran army horses turned out on the Forest.

The first outside stallion of real merit to be introduced to the Forest breed in the 18th century was Marske, the sire of Eclipse, owned by Butcher Cumberland, then Lord Warden of the Forest. On Cumberland's death, Marske was sold to a farmer living near Ringwood where he covered 'country' mares. When Eclipse showed his outstanding ability Marske was whisked away to higher things in Oxfordshire. He was 19 by then and could only have got to Oxfordshire on his own hooves so he certainly had stamina. He continued to get foals, but not another Eclipse.

William Gilpin in *Remarks on Forest Scenery 1791* has an etching of New Forest ponies described as follows:

> The New Forest horse is often supposed to be of Spanish extraction, imagined to have been shipwrecked on the coast of Hamshire from the Armada, but I look on this as a species of the ancient vaunt Genus a Jove ummo and to deserve as little attention. Some of them have a form, which would not disgrace so noble a lineage. The grey horse represented is among the most beautiful.

But in general, the croup of the Forest horse is low, and his head ill set on, having what the jockeys call stiff jaw (and Glenda Spooner very much later described as swallowing the poker).

Of this defect the resemblance is given in the horse on the left (*in the picture*), who's head is set on as those of the Forest commonly are. Their claim therefor to high lineage must, in general rest more on their good qualities, than on beauty, on the hardiness of their nature, on their uncommon strength, on their agility and sureness of foot, which they probably acquire by constantly lifting their legs among furze. But tho the form of the New Forest horse is seldom beautiful; yet as the ornament of a Forest scene, he is very picturesque. The horse in his natural state, rough with his mane about him and his tail waving in the wind as he feeds, is always beautiful, but particularly in so wild a scene as this, which he graces exceedingly.

Deputy Surveyor Cumberbatch in the 19th century, wishing to implement the rolling enclosure powers whereby, as one lot of trees grew big enough not to be eaten by grazing animals, that area was thrown open and another enclosed for timber growing, tried to reduce the value of Commoners' rights by proposing to introduce 'winter heyning' (prohibiting winter grazing) which appears never to have been applied to the Forest. Knowing this would be unpopular, he sought a sweetener and in 1852 borrowed an Arab stallion Zorah, from the Prince Consort, to stand in New Park (Crown freehold enclosed land in the middle of the Forest where the New Forest County Show is held; stallions are now run on it in winter and there is a polo ground.) The Commoners saw through the plot and also did not wish to disturb the mares' haunting by taking them to New Park. Zorah was therefore not well supported and what foals he did get, if they were better than their dams, were sold and if not so good were turned back to breed. After four years he got sick requiring the attentions of the most expensive vet in Southampton. Mr Cumberbatch concluded he was not a very good horse anyway so on his recovery he was sent back to Windsor by train.

Good ponies were in demand in the 19th century and many good ponies, mainly colts, were sold off the Forest. One such was Squib, foaled in 1814; although under 12.0hh, she is said to have covered 20 miles in one hour and a quarter, and 3 miles in 8 minutes. (Garth Starflower covered 3 miles in 6 minutes 20 seconds. She stood 13.0hh and was carrying 11stone 2lb). Squib is described as 'having a fairly large but remarkably eastern type of head, a rather short neck, dropping and rather narrow quarters, high on the hock, light of bone but a good shoulder and great depth through the heart, with docility, courage and speed.' Mr Dale in Vol. 1 NFPSB (New Forest Pony Stud Book) 1910 said she might stand as a portrait of a pony at that time; she was incidentally another grey. Her description haunted us by being read out as the breed description at every major show throughout the 1950s.

2
ARCHITECTS OF THE FOREST

THE VERY CLOSE GRAZING AND BROWSING of the ponies is essential for the survival of certain plants and insects, including butterflies and some birds. The pasture woodlands have little understorey and a very pronounced browse line, particularly of holly. In the Forest holly grows into tall trees; elsewhere it is usually only a shrub. The upper part often has no prickles but when it snows the weight of the snow bends these branches down and allows them to be browsed just when they are most needed. Holly starts very tight and prickly and with bramble protects young saplings, but as it grows it becomes more openwork and the ponies can then eat it. With age it becomes thin but pollarding will rejuvenate it and it will come again from the root, making it nearly everlasting.

Traditional management of the heath by burning in the early months of the year encourages the grass to come rather earlier; the young growth of heather is a much more valuable food than the old and old gorse becomes open and woody and so no use for shelter, birds' nests or feed whilst the regrowth is extremely valuable. Gorse is a legume, relatively high in protein and has the ability to take nitrogen from the air to fertilize the soil. Ponies also always go and nip off the ends of the burnt gorse shoots. They have a natty way of eating gorse without getting pricked and some grow moustaches to help. Because of their grazing and browsing, the ponies have been called the 'architects of the Forest'.

Mediaeval villages were usually surrounded by woods and manor wasteland over which villagers had rights to graze stock, collect fuel and bracken for bedding cattle, and turn out pigs in the autumn to clear up acorns that poison ponies and cattle. It is not known whether the common rights were just the usual practice or whether they were granted to compensate for villagers not being allowed to erect a fence high enough to impede the passage of the King's deer. The Forest was originally designated an area where deer were protected by fierce Forest laws to provide a supply of fresh meat in winter for the Court, handy while they waited for the wind to change to let them sail to Normandy.

Forest pony eating gorse.

The Court consisted of a relatively large number of unproductive feed producers.

NATIVE PONY ADAPTATION

All native ponies have much in common and some special adaptations. All need to conserve energy to survive the lean months of winter when grass does not grow; for this they need a relatively deep body and short cannons. Since there is no flesh below the knees and hocks, blood vessels are close under the skin so the longer the cannon the greater the heat loss. All have wonderfully waterproof coats with whorls placed to throw off the rain and hairs that stand up to trap air like a string vest. They have a spread of hair at the top of the tail to act as an umbrella when they turn their backs to the wind and rain; a tuft of feather directs water away from the heels and a heavy mane helps keep the blood warm on its rather long journey to the brain and also protects the neck when stallions fight or grab the mare to hold her still for serving. A good depth of jaw allows a long tooth root and ensures the teeth stay firmly together as they wear. Most native ponies have small ears but Forest ponies often have very long ones, for in a Forest hearing is an even more important sense than sight for getting warning of predators. Most important of all is tolerance to local parasites. This tolerance is probably why the Commoners requested the Stud Book be closed to outside blood because 'those with the most old Forest blood stayed longest on the Forest'. The Exmoors running at Ferneycroft at that time just before the Great War did not do very well, neither did the Foresters turned out on Exmoor.

Native ponies are tough and hardy, which makes them relatively cheap to keep. Many never need shoeing because they move straight and wear their feet evenly: useful in free-running ponies who never see a farrier. They are self-willed, because they have had to look after themselves, but this often means also looking after their riders. Forest-bred ponies are very 'street wise': when it comes to being broken in they have been through water and seen the plastic bag in the bush, they have been over ditches and narrow bridges and are usually traffic-proof. This indeed is often their undoing as, once used to traffic, they completely ignore it. The motorist thinks that because they must be able to see him they will get out of his way, but, no, even if he sounds his horn, they cross the road anyway with disastrous results. About 100 ponies a year are killed on Forest roads. When the speed limit was first introduced animal accidents fell by a third and human ones by half! Alas, speed crept up and so did the casualties.

SOCIAL LIFE

Most herds consist of just two or three mares and their daughters, very few areas have enough keep for large herds. The stallion moves between several small groups who join and split frequently, some mares will cover considerable distances to find a mate but most mares stay on the same haunt all their lives. Some stallions drive out fillies, but these tend to sneak back: is this a way of avoiding in-breeding? All stallions drive out colts who then form bachelor groups which graze the poorer areas and rear up to eat leaves.

The herd leader is always an older mare, who knows where the fresh water, shelter, seasonal feed and escape routes are. The stallion brings up the rear to chase up stragglers with the typical 'snakey' low head movement. Fights are usually tests of dominance, rearing up and catching the other fellow's neck to try and bring him to his knees. They cannot afford to get hurt so the weaker generally soon runs away, to live to fight another day. Occasionally, while a fight is in progress a third

Shading.

stallion sneaks in and steals a mare. Most stallions seem to prefer to stay with mares they know; they will serve maiden mares until their regular partners are receptive but then often lose interest in newcomers. Late in the season the members of several herds quite often shade together and the stallions may move away from their ladies. Some however cover considerable distances going round several small herds if there is not enough grazing to round up a large herd in one place.

Mares usually foal in May – very early – or foals born after early June are a drain on the mares, who need to foal when the grass is at its best. Mares usually go off to foal alone and at night, but return to the herd as soon as the foal is up and running and can recognize its dam. Foals not removed in the autumn continue to suckle all winter which is a great strain on the mare particularly if she is in-foal again.

FEED

To survive on the moors in winter they pile on the fat when food is available, which makes them prone to laminitis when kept in. On the moor the fat layer is the winter food reserve. Perhaps some insects have been put on this earth to prevent ponies getting too fat, for when they get too irritating the ponies stop eating and 'shade, standing head to tail, switching each other's flies off.' There are traditional shades, sometimes under trees, but often in the open where there is a little breeze; but ponies are opportunists and have learnt petrol and diesel fumes keep off flies. This encourages them onto the roads and into the villages. Here visitors offer them tit-bits which leads to jealousy. One pony sees another being fed and dives in to chase the first one off and claim her share of any goodies; people then get knocked over and may be bitten or kicked; the pony then has to be moved from its natural haunt and chosen company or removed altogether. Over the years this policy has led to generally a very docile breed but many potentially excellent animals with perhaps more sparkle have been lost. Salt put on the roads in winter also attracts stock to the roads at the most dangerous period and the run off from alkaline road chippings makes verge grazing sweet.

Native ponies on their native heaths have the advantage of a high fibre diet, so they grow slowly. They have plenty of space and varied terrain to gallop over so their joints and bones are stressed without weight on their backs: shown to be important for long-term soundness. Those bred in the same area for several generations build up a tolerance to the local parasites so they can hold condition even with quite a worm burden. In the Forest we have crab flies, our local secret weapon; Forest-bred ponies have developed tolerance and ignore their tickling (they tickle between the back legs and under the tail but do not actually bite) but ponies from outside go mental. In a show class where one gets loose the Foresters stand quietly while the outsider kicks and almost throws itself to the ground.

It is very noticeable that ponies do best in a dry year. Not only do they hate perpetual rain but when conditions are dry they can get onto land usually too boggy where there is fresh grazing; this takes them off the dryer, but now burnt-up acid grasslands, which get a rest. This helps reduce the worm count. Ponies are often seen eating dead leaves, not because they are starving but because deep rooted trees bring up essential minerals from the subsoil and drop 90% of them in their leaf litter. Whilst most but certainly not all ponies avoid ragwort and even the grass round it, acorns are very popular and can be just as deadly, building up over time to destroy the liver, just like alcohol in humans. As with drink, it often starts by making the ponies fat, so some ripe acorns fatten for the winter, but green ones or too many send them mad; I have seen a pony charge over glass cloches; quite a few get addicted and will eat nothing else when acorns are available and there are thousands of oak trees in the Forest and in the hedges of the holdings.

Far more ponies die of acorns than ragwort in the Forest. With the huge reduction in stallion numbers and the fact that herds are not completely separated, there is interaction between the Forest running ponies and some studs which makes the ponies very vulnerable both to gene loss and to infectious disease. Gene loss because of the small proportion of male to female. Gene variety encourages adaptability and, since conditions are always changing, gene loss will lead to extinction.

3
TYPE

SO WHAT IS TRUE TO TYPE? First and foremost the pony must be a true pony type and not a small horse. Pony characteristics, as defined by Lord Lucas, are:

> There is a certain quality in ponies which entirely distinguishes them from horses - "pony character". It is almost more mental than physical. It is, as the name conveys, more a question of character than size, make or shape. A pony can be bigger than a cob, yet a true cob has horse character and a pony has pony character, it is one of the first things a judge looks for and of its importance every judge is agreed. I believe it is a combination of many things, none of them, except the head, being purely physical. It is that which enables a pony to live where a horse would starve, to trot over ground where a horse would walk, to thrive on work that would kill a horse, of equal strength, to be clever where a horse would be stupid, to be a friend where a horse would be a servant, all these and a thousand other similar attributes are comprised in "pony character". If we are to breed ponies we cannot afford to risk anything that would lose it, for it can be lost. A few crosses with a horse, although he himself be of pony origin, will soon destroy or completely impair it.

He thought 'these characteristics will be well known to the owner, who should consider them when deciding breeding policy'. Other physical points that can be considered by a judge include good width between the eyes, to allow room for a brain; the pony should be slightly longer from point of shoulder to back of buttocks than high at the withers; depth of body should about equal length of leg with the cannons considerably shorter than the forearm. This is an energy conserving shape necessary for wintering on the moors. The pony should have dense bone, shown by being well defined, as should the joints with the knees flat. The pony should have vitality, striding out and really covering the ground, tracking up at walk as well as trot. The movement has evolved from the terrain where the ponies live and the uses to which they have been put. The terrain is rough so some, but not too much knee action is required. If the pony moved with the low, straight limbed, daisy cutting action of the show pony he would trip up on the moor. Ponies have always

Wayland Cranberry, Breed Supreme Champion, 2004, ridden by Elaine Morgan: a larger pony.

Farrier's Drummer Boy, a small under 13.2hh pony but the same type.

been maids of all work, which gives them their great versatility but colt hunting has long been the local sport and ask Commoners how they wish to celebrate anything from the millennium to Queen Victoria's golden jubilee and they always say with pony races. Forest ponies have been raced for hundreds of years, in the 18th and 19th centuries both trotting and galloping, so a fast pony has always been appreciated and this causes a dilemma. Long cannons make for speed particularly with shallow bodies, but this type is not so hardy or weight-carrying, which has led to welfare problems. Originally the fastest ponies would have escaped the wolves. The solution is to start the movement with the shoulders and hips, which gives length of stride and power; the pony must really use its shoulders and hocks, not move only from the elbows. The movement should be free, loose, elastic, athletic and rhythmic; walk four time, trot two time, canter three time and gallop four time, and this gallop can only be achieved by letting the pony stretch his neck and really lengthen. The breed description says the movement should be straight but not exaggerated; Welsh ponies, being natural showmen, should have more exaggerated movement than Foresters. Many youngsters go very close in walk but less so in trot; provided they do not actually knock fetlocks

Willoway Pipers Paragon, owned by Mrs Shorey, ridden by M. Shorey: Olympia qualifier: another smaller pony.

or plait this can be forgiven, it usually improves as the pony gains more muscle. They justly have a reputation for good temperament, probably, after soundness, the most important consideration when breeding but again not often possible to judge on a few minutes' viewing.

How do Forest ponies differ from Connemaras? Some say a Conny looks up and a Forester down but this is not universal. Connys are usually broader and rounder over the withers and usually have a more curved lower jaw to neck set. This sometimes makes the Forester look inadequate beside them but has two advantages: children's legs are not so stretched so they can sit better and the narrower back is kinder to elderly people's backs.

It is interesting to note that measuring colts' bone below the knee shows some ponies increase a whole inch in circumference between two and five years of age. The smallest ponies never had less than 6½ inches at two years, the bigger 8 to 9 inches. Those that were light of bone were usually in the middle section.

VERSATILITY

New Forest ponies are extremely versatile. Horses have been bred for specialist jobs for generations but ponies did all the work in their native areas. Father inspecting stock on the moors and rounding them up rode them; if they were lucky, the children might ride them to school or for pleasure. The pony would bring home the hay, bracken for bedding the cattle, and peat and wood for fuel. He would also take the family to church and to market and would harrow the fields. Forest ponies have always been raced.

When compiling an exhibition of versatile NF ponies we came up with 36 different activities. When long distance riding started, Beelzebub won a Bronze in the Golden Horseshoe and Beacon Periwinkle qualified at 8.4mph over 40 miles but was not allowed to go to the final as she was only 13.2hh and the minimum height was 14.0hh.

The Enthusiasts Riding Club has entered teams for riding club competitions for dressage, and jumping and has often been placed at the finals. They entered and won a novice team chase and had two

Wainsford Wonderful Surprise

medal winning ponies at a Pony Dressage International in Ireland. Forest ponies have frequently been in Continental international teams. Indeed the top performance pony stallion for some years was a New Forest pony Møehlerons Tajo by Peveril Probus a stud bred stallion from a Forest bred mare.

The Enthusiasts Stallion Musical Ride performed all round the country, notably in Hyde Park at the Country Festival where one night a small black Forester was substituted for a Life Guards horse. Over the years 39 stallions took part often travelling together and being tied together on the side of the lorry. Once during rehearsal in an indoor school one tried to fight himself in the mirror but otherwise there were no untoward incidents.

Two ponies have been placed in BHS One Day Events, both being 8

Mavis Garrett on Limekiln Wildeye barrel racing.

James Haynes clearing a jump at Lymington Horse Show in the late '50s.

inches smaller than every other competitor. Tildiz Tobacco Leaf has won Western competitions, goes under side saddle, in harness and jumps. Many have been used for RDA riding and driving. They are often children's ponies but kept on to do adult competitions. Some have been in Pony Club teams for one-day events, jumping and dressage and one 11.3hh Prince Philip Cup pony won a chase-me-charlie competition at 4 feet. In the latest competitions, Le Trec and Barrel Racing, they do well.

Most jump well: Rushmoor Sunrise has won many open working hunter pony classes including 2nd place at the Horse of the Year Show where Silverlea Rosencavalier won the BSJA 138cm class in 2002. Other ponies have played polo and many are excellent colt hunting and hunting ponies.

During the war when horse blood to grow Tetanus vaccine could not be imported some Commoners earned an honest penny by allowing their ponies to be blood donors. Holland now has a herd used to provide milk for children who cannot have cows' milk, they were chosen for their docility and because they are good milkers. They are also used for conservation grazing, as well as the more usual Pony Club, gymkhanas, etc. They have certainly proved themselves.

Native ponies have a low boredom level and need plenty of

Gail Brownrigg riding Tildiz Tobacco Leaf.

stimulation; most problems occur when they have not got enough to do; regular varied work is the answer. Unlike horses who like the same food at the same time every day, ponies like variety; in the wild the same plants are not available all the year round. Too much of the same rye grass hay and they can be very picky: meadow hay with a variety of plants included is much more popular. They have excellent, very long memories, which they need to recognize plants that do not grow every year. For example, one old mare thought the gateway from her field was too muddy so she went and stood where the gate used to be twenty years before. She had not been lunged for about twenty years; when an instructor wanted to give a disabled rider a lesson on the lunge, as soon as the long rein was attached she knew exactly what was required. Of course they also remember bad experiences.

New Forest ponies have proved themselves essential to the survival of the traditional character of the New Forest. They have the adaptability, temperament, athleticism, conformation and movement to compete successfully in any discipline and the strength and stamina to be real family ponies for all aged riders. However as most are bred in and around the Forest they are very vulnerable to the possible introduction of new diseases; with a very small percentage of stallions and the inability to totally separate herds, they are vulnerable to gene loss. With the present way of life where ponies are boxed to rallies and competitions and ridden for relatively short periods at a time there is a danger of losing stamina. The trend to taller, longer legged sports ponies endangers type; foals, sometimes reared on their own, in very small paddocks are also in danger of losing stamina.

In 2005 at the Riding Club Dressage to music the stallion Farriers Fingerprint, substituted at short notice to partner Farriers Foxglove in the pairs, was 2nd between two pairs of horses in spite of being different colours whilst Wayland Cranberry was 9th overall.

New Forest ponies have had some unusual jobs - one was used in his work by a gamekeeper, another by a rural policeman to patrol his beat.

Matley Merlin II, a Forest bred pony sold as a foal at Beaulieu Rd sales, won the 2005 Pony Club winter Jumping Championship, a nationwide competition where ponies have to come through two qualifying rounds; about 80 ponies qualify and the standard is high. Beacon Pieris won the style and performance cup. Since the results came out in *Horse and Hound* with a good write up there has been considerable interest in the sales.

Wayland Loganberry was accepted as a sports pony stallion in 2005.

The latest activity reported is that New Forest ponies are taking part in Pony Club racing.

4

VERDERER'S COURT & SOCIETIES

THIS ANCIENT FOREST COURT WAS ORIGINALLY SET UP to protect the king's deer and the 'verd' (green) that they eat. The court was reconstituted in 1949 and now has 5 members elected by those who occupy at least one acre of land with common rights; the same qualification is required to stand for election, and members are appointed by DEFRA, the Forestry Commission, the planning authority and the Countryside Commission, with an Official Verderer appointed by the Queen on the Forestry Commission's recommendation. The problem is Commoners have to get themselves onto the electoral roll for every election (every three years) and a lot fail to do so. The court is charged with managing commoning and protecting the grazing and is a statutory body which holds the definitive atlas of common rights drawn up in 1852 when the Office of Woods tried to disallow as many rights as possible.

The large landowners registered all their land, some well away from the open Forest, whilst some smallholders missed out and a lot of land was considered to have been illegally enclosed. In theory very little can happen on the open Forest without the consent of the Verderers who have a good record of preserving it from various inroads such as oil exploitation and a bypass that would have gone right out into the Forest. They can make bylaws and control stallions. They employ the Agisters to look after the stock on the open Forest. At present there are five, a senior Agister and four others; each has an area but with holidays, etc, they need a good knowledge of the whole Forest. They are the unfortunate chaps called out to road accidents in the middle of cold, wet winter nights to try and find a possibly badly injured pony who could have gone quite a way. They also have to deal with cows who calve while their owners are at work, angry people who have their beautiful gardens invaded by pigs; donkeys with overgrown feet; anything that is sick, injured, stuck in a bog or who has got onto a main road or railway; they also collect the marking fees due on all stock turned out on the Forest and they organize the annual drifts. These are round-ups where Commoners assist in driving ponies into the pounds so that they can be recorded and tail marked; foals for sale are removed

Drift; rider Colin Moore.

with any mares not likely to winter well and foals that are being kept are branded; some ponies are wormed and have collars fitted to make them visible in the dark and some need attention to their feet.

Sometimes they get an amusing assignment such as the sow who was spotted going the wrong way down a one-way route and who turned into the District Offices where the automatic door opened for her. By the time the Agister arrived the staff had swept her into the bicycle shed.

The Verderers control stallions who run out with annual inspections of those already registered and licensed by the Pony Society. There is also a bylaw to enforce the removal of coming two-year-old colts, at the moment by February 1st, until they have been passed and licensed. To avoid late foals and cut the number of foals, in 2001 the number of stallions passed was cut from 90 to 34 and they were only allowed to run out for 8 weeks. The reduced number of foals at the sales and

Early 20th century Commoners leaving a drift with ponies tied round their riding ponies' necks.

the addition of a foal show where foals had to be halter broken, which encouraged new private buyers, did improve prices somewhat. Stallion owners were not happy with the short time they were allowed out and, in spite of being offered grazing for them in New Park, insisted on being allowed to turn them out from February to mid July, a decision not popular with some mare owners who fear very early foals. All stallions are moved to a different area to avoid inbreeding after three years, not that they always stay put! In 2005 two areas at New Park and Cadland Estate have been found so all stallions can be kept off the open Forest until March 31st.

From 2004 the Verderers are administering a scheme that acknowledges the value of the grazing done by Commoners' animals by paying a headage fee for those turned out, but with a limit on numbers.

By 1880 it was generally considered the stock had deteriorated: whilst there were a number of good mares the stallions were deplorable. Since good colts sold well, most were sold, on the grounds that if a good price were refused when offered the pony would probably break its leg in a rabbit hole or drown in a bog and the owner would be left with nothing.

Those worth nothing were left to breed. However during the Boer War in South Africa the Forest Scouts (a locally raised detachment) took their ponies who survived the long route marches carrying 15 stone better than the regular remounts and on their return won an army jumping competition at Aldershot in spite of it looking as if the riders would knock down the jumps with their feet.

At this time it was thought the ponies were in-bred and outside blood was needed. (Recent computer studies show a significant amount of in-breeding was unlikely, under natural conditions nature takes care of her own. Selection by selling the best colts was surely the trouble.) There was no inducement to keep a good stallion since there was no chance of getting stud fees and no guarantee he would run with his owner's mares. In May 1887 the Verderers decided to hire three stallions to improve the breed; the next year it increased to four: **Fitz George**, Mr Mill's **Welsh Star**, **Katerfelto** and **Bampton Boy**. There was not much demand for Bampton Boy's services. Katerfelto served 47 mares getting 29 foals, 13 colts and 16 fillies, 6 mares slipped. Welsh Star got 16 foals from 23 mares, Fitz George got 18 colts, 9 fillies, 19 mares slipped! After the Deputy Surveyor reminded the Court that for many years both stallions and mares had been maintained in New Park by

A Forest Scout, one of the team that won the inter services jumping competition at Aldershot on their return from South Africa, where they routinely carried 13 stone on long route marches.

the Crown, Queen Victoria was persuaded to lend two Arab stallions, Abeyan and Yuresson, but the Commoners did not like the scheme, preferring prizes or premiums to stallions that ran out.

The Verderers therefore stopped financing the idea, which was taken over by the Four Ponies Scheme, founded in 1890 by certain Verderers and others. The idea was to stand one stallion in a field in each of the four Agisters districts and to run stallions on the Forest in season keeping them in in the winter. It was estimated there were 2,000-3,000 mares on the Forest and a similar number in work on the holdings, many of which were bred from.

The Four Ponies Society

The Four Ponies Society was founded in 1890 to run for four years and its final report in 1894 says it all:

'The Four Ponies Scheme, the report of which is hereby made on its termination, was founded in 1890 by a guaranteed yearly subscription of those gentlemen forming the Court of Verderers of the New Forest and others who joined in this work for a term of four years for purpose of purchasing and keeping four suitable stallions in hand or to run in the Forest for the improvement of the breed of New Forest ponies; so as to continue the good work commenced by the Court of Verderers by the hire of four stallions of a good stamp. These subscriptions and some donations to a total amount of £276.9.6.has been expended, the assets now being four pony stallions ,viz. Sprig of Shillelagh II, Exmoor, West Highlander and Brockenhurst Joe.

The loan of two pure bred Arab stallions, Abeyan and Yuresson, by Her Most Gracious Majesty the Queen has greatly assisted the work of the Four-Pony Scheme.

These stallions were most kindly kept in hand and cared for, free of cost by the Right Honourable Lord Montague of Beaulieu, and David Jones Esq. of Warbourne. The produce of Abeyan particularly proved of great value, affording a strain of a hardy stamp with plenty of bone, which will for long be traced in the District. These two Arabs were returned to Windsor in the autumn of 1893 with the hearty thanks of the subscribers.

NOTE

Abeyan Vol.1 NPS stud Book, bay, little white on legs, star, Anazt tribe from north Arabia, 19 yrs old when imported in 1885. Yuresson had a few foals registered in Vol.1 NFPBSB as did Katerfelto but there are a number of spelling variations which make it difficult to know if they are all the same pony.

Illingworth at the end of the 20th century recommended 2500 – 3000 ponies were necessary for the conservation of the Forest.

J.C.Tinne Esq; of Bashley Manor also was good enough to help the scheme by the presentation of Brockenhurst Joe, whose services running in the Forest have been greatly appreciated. Sprig of Shillelagh II, an Irish Steeple-chasing pony, grandson of Stockwell, was purchased in 1890 for £75. Exmoor, Blue Roan, Hebridean and West Highlander in 1891. Sprig of Shillelagh II has up to the present time been most kindly kept in hand free of charge by Sir George Meyrick Esq; and Exmoor, Blue Roan, Hebridean and Brockenhurst Joe, have been run in various quarters of the Forest since their acquirement being taken in and kept in pasture etc. during the winter season. Blue Roan and Hebridean both died in the Forest in the early autumn of 1892, having done good service (was 1892 a good acorn year?) thus leaving, as above stated, Sprig of Shillelagh, Exmoor, West Highlander, and Brockenhurst Joe to represent the stallion stock in hand at the close of the four years for which the subscriptions were guaranteed. It is recommended Sprig of Shillelagh be sold as soon as convenient, Mr. Meyrick being unable to continue the charge of him. On 10.2.94. the Four Ponies Scheme was, with the consent of the subscribers and by a resolution of the New Forest Pony Association, affiliated to the latter, and it has been managed by a committee appointed for that purpose. It is satisfactory to be able to state that at the present time a very great improvement has taken place in the New Forest ponies, which is confirmed by the remarks of all that were present at the late Pony Fair at Lyndhurst held on the 9th August. This result cannot but be most gratifying and satisfactory to those who by their subscriptions and exertions have worked to this end, and it is trusted that this improvement to the New Forest ponies will be appreciated by and of value to the Commoners and other breeders who own the same as well as those who eventually use Foresters for pleasure or profit.

There can be no doubt that the continuance of the system of premiums granted at the Annual April Stallion Shows of the New Forest Pony Association is absolutely necessary to continue the work commenced by the Court of Verderers in 1887 and continued by the Four Ponies Scheme to the present time, but which now ceases.

It is trusted that, should the above four pony stallions be transferred to the New Forest Pony Association, it will be found possible to continue the services of four suitable stallions being run in the Forest in the season.

The Society for the Improvement of New Forest Ponies was set up in February 1891 to run a spring Stallion Show to award premiums to stallions that ran the Forest as the Commoners had requested. It later became known as the Lyndhurst Society, and the Four Pony Scheme amalgamated with it. Unfortunately the first minute book is missing, and until the Burley and District New Forest Breeding and Cattle Society (Burley Society) was founded in 1906 and started a Stud Book, early show records are uninformative. In many cases they just say:

'Mr So and So's bay yearling'; so was his bay 2-year-old the following year the same pony?

The Council for the 1891 Society consisted of a President, Lord Montague, at least two Vice Presidents, Lord Manners and the Earl of Normanton, Sir George Thursby, MBH(Master of Buckhounds), and Sir George Meyrick, MFH, Col. Cornwallis West, MP, Walter Gilby Esq.; 8 Landowning Commoners, 8 Commoners, being pony owners, 4 resident non-Commoners and 4 non-resident non-Commoners. These were F. Lovell, Col. Esdaile, Major Talbot, Mr V. Pinhorn, Mr W. Domeny, George Meyrick, Esq; G. E. Matcham, Esq., G. Briscoe Eyre, Esq., Mr J. Burden, MRCVS, Mr H. Saunders, The Hon. J. Scott Montague, W. Meons, Esq., the Hon. G. Lascelles (Deputy Surveyor), R. Morton Peto, Esq., Capt. Standish, Mr F. Strange, Mr. G. Golden, Mr. E. Bramble, and Mr. H. Wort. Hon.; Solicitor G. Mortimer, Esq., Hon. Treasurer D. Jones Esq., Hon. Secretaries R. Blathwayt and Mr A.Higham.

A Stallion Show was to be held each April, or such other time as the Council should decide, for members' ponies. The minimum subscription was 5/- (it went down to 2/6 between the wars and only above 5/- in 1966!). The subscription included all entry fees for the show (in 1909 of 84 ponies entered 50 belonged to just 3 owners who certainly got their money's worth.) Prizes and premiums only to be paid on a certificate from the Agister, with the consent of the Verderers that the stallion had been running out on the Forest from the date fixed by the Council until the following August. All stallions gaining premiums to be recommended to the Verderers to be passed and marked to run the Forest. (This was soon changed to only those stallions passed by the Verderers being eligible to go forward to be judged for premiums.) No stallion to take a premium for more than six years. Youngstock premiums only to be paid when the pony had run out as a three-year-old. Each stallion to be examined and passed by the assisting Veterinary Surgeon as to soundness; Ministry Licence defects to be looked for (at the time a number of conditions now unacceptable were not included, such as parrot mouth and sweet itch for example, eyes were not looked into and the examination was pretty superficial; I have seen the vet pass a pony through field glasses from the other side of the bog). All stallions of Russian or Polish blood to be disallowed! Were they fashionable? Judges to be two Council Members who were also Verderers, two Council members who represent quarters of the

Release after drift.

Forest as pony breeders and one non-Commoner assisted by a vet. We are lucky that the Verderers were given control of stallions under the 1877 New Forest Act. Two of the judges officiated for twenty years. No judge could enter a pony at the show.

The silver cup presented by Mr Purkins in 1898 was won outright by Lord Arthur Cecil's Lord Ebrington (the pony was given his breeder's name), an improved Exmoor who ran at Decoy Pond till 1902. Ten Exmoor mares ran at Ferneycroft as an experiment but did not winter any better than many other ponies. By 1909 judges had been reduced to two and it was felt necessary to include in the show catalogue: 'The Council again desire to state that the Verderers assisted by their Veterinary Surgeon Mr Goodall alone pass as sound the stallions to run on the Forest and that the Association has nothing to do with this business, the ponies being only judged when they have passed.' Obviously some rather sensitive toes had again been trodden on.

Once the Burley Society's Stud Book started it was agreed all stallions awarded a premium should be entered in it. No pony docked after 1909 was passed; since the docking act was not passed for many years, this was very foresighted. At the 1896 show, 35 out of the 46 animals contesting the class for ponies 4 years and over were bred on the Forest, and these were considered to have kept better condition on the Forest than the imported ponies although the Commoners liked the Exmoors because a bay/brown with mealy muzzle was considered to be the good old Forest type. This had been lost partly in the attempt to gain height and bone so the ponies could be used for draught; coarse round bone and common heads had been an unintended result. With mechanization these animals were no longer required and the hairy heels have largely gone but we still have some round bone and horsey heads.

The judges report for 1901 survives and reads: ' Yearlings, the winner of the medal in this class showed a touch of Arab blood, 42 animals contested the class for 4 yrs and upwards, taken as a whole they showed a remarkable evenness in both quality and condition so the competition for the 20 premiums of £2 was keen, 16 three-year-olds competed, 10 were awarded premiums. Several of these ponies, considering their age, came out remarkably well. Two-year-olds were well supported: for 15 premiums there were 21 entries, all looked promising. It may be of interest that there were 26 brown ponies, 19 bay, 14 grey, 14 black, 9 roan, 3 chestnut and 1 dun. Mature and broken ponies were also at the show. The Society being short of cash it was proposed that races be held at the stallion show and in 1913 that each master of hounds that hunted the Forest be asked to hold a cap in April when the visitors came to hunt in the Forest.

Royal Commission 1912

A Royal Commission was set up in 1912 to look into the state of British Mountain and Moorland ponies which it defined as: 'one whose ancestors had lived on mountain, moor or common for the last three generations in a semi-feral condition'. Their terms of reference were to:

1. Consider the value of M&M ponies in relation to other breeds.
2. The best methods of giving assistance.
3. The most practical way to assist the small owner: marketing, cost of transport and state of the pasture.
4. Preserve breed purity.
5. The advisability of a change of blood to avoid inbreeding.

They concluded M&M ponies were the foundation of all light horses in the country including Thoroughbreds and so were extremely important foundation stocks. They stressed the importance of

Agisters in their heyday:(left to right) *Albert Evemy, Charles Evemy and Jessie Taylor, 1910.*

registration in recognised stud books and of associations in each district. They recommended that the best method of help was to award premiums to stallions, mares and youngstock.

On marketing they noted prices at Lyndhurst Fair: brood mares £8-£9, broken ponies averaged £25, top price £50, yearlings £5-£10, 3-year-olds £10 -£15. Transport costs by rail were 25% above those for cattle, nonetheless 61 ponies travelled from Brockenhurst to Canterbury for £17.9.6.

With regard to the pasture it was reported:

1. Seedling firs are over running the Forest, the Crown refuses to exterminate them.

2. The Crown does not burn enough heather and gorse and will not allow anyone else to do so.

3. Motorists kill many cattle and ponies.

4. Fences, deer, gates and stock gates have fallen into disrepair allowing lane creeping and subsequent fines to the owners.

5. The removal of deer disturbed the feeding cycle and ruined the

pasture, deer cleared undergrowth, ponies followed deer, and cattle ponies, each preparing the land for the others, now scrub covers lawns, there are thousands of firs where there were none, particularly on Beaulieu Heath and Burley Lawn to the Rifle Butts.

They recommended 6 premiums be awarded to registered M&M stallions brought to the show. They should be judged by someone appointed by the Board of Agriculture, who would provide the cash; they would then be awarded a district to run from May 15th to August 1st, though there could be difficulties in getting them to stay where they were put! They further recommended the Commons Act be enforced to remove unfit stock.

The report was sent by his masters to the Deputy Surveyor for his comments. Mr Lascelles replied:

Sir,

I have the honour to return certain papers relating to pony breeding on Dartmoor which have been referred to me for my observations, presumably as to New Forest for I know nothing about Dartmoor!

The control of the Commoners rights and of the turning out of ponies in the Forest is now vested in the Court of Verderers. They have power to regulate the turning out of stallions, and what is even more important to exclude immature and inferior stallions from being turned out.

As to the importance of this, I entirely agree with what is said by Lord Arthur Cecil and Mr Pease. But the Verderers do not make as full use of their powers as they might and are disposed generally to yield to the clamour of the commoners and allow any cheap worthless animal, which they have no convenience for keeping at home, to run out. As to improvement of New Forest ponies, the number being turned out and the persons who breed them seemed to have considerably decreased of late years and it is quite certain that both the number and quality of the ponies brought to the local Fairs for sale has greatly deteriorated during the last ten years.

But it is fact that Lord Arthur Cecil and one or two other persons have gone in largely for pony breeding as a speculation during the last ten years or so, and have imported and turned out various stallions of several different breeds in the New Forest. Thus it is the fact and this fact is highly advertised, that a limited number of persons are breeding in the New Forest a number of ponies of better stamp than used formerly to be bred, except by a very small number of persons. Consequently at the shows held by the pony Association, which is a rather closed borough, there are exhibited sundry better class ponies, bred by some half dozen owners, and the breed is said, but erroneously to have improved. There are some better ponies bred in the Forest than there used to be and

Rose Water, grandsire of Field Marshall foaled 1881.

better stallions are available; but the rank and file of breeders and of ponies are not one bit improved and are not likely to be so, because the one idea of the New Forest Commoner is to produce something to sell; what ever it is, it must be all profit for he will risk nothing. Hence he greatly resents it if he is prevented from turning out a two year old stallion that would give him some trouble or eat some forage at home, and in this way, just as on Dartmoor the general run of breeders are opposed to improvement rather than inclined to support it. The greater number of ponies are no better than of yore, many are worse. It is of no use to attempt to improve the breed of anything by turning out better sires unless the inferior ones are excluded. And this is recognised by the correspondents of the Board of Agriculture. A good deal might be done in this direction if the Verderers would summon up the courage to do it; but they are an elective body and likely to deem it more in their interest to please their constituents than improve ponies.

Yours etc

Because Lascelles was sent the wrong section it allowed him to ignore the criticism of the state of the pasture.

In defence of the Verderers it has to be said that the annual sale of foals

Field Marshall.

was an important part of a Commoners' income: no foal, no income, so it was necessary to pass enough stallions to cover the mares. Not less than 80 mature stallions were considered necessary. Some would be passed because no other horse would stay in a particular place, and of course the Verderers could only pass what was shown to them, often not a very good lot of ponies. A Commoner could not guarantee his stallion would run with his mares and he got no benefit at all if it did not. In any case after three years it would be moved to avoid it covering its own daughters. In those days no horse could take more than 6 premiums and no horse could run out after the age of 18 years; he could be ordered off at any time if considered mischievous. A good gelding made a good price whereas a stallion on the Forest was vulnerable to being beaten up by a rival, killed by a car or breaking a leg in a rabbit hole, etc. Thus there was little incentive to keep a stallion.

True wild horses do not breed till they are mature at 6 years, but this is a long time to wait for any financial return, so Commoners tended to sell as barren, mares who had not had a foal by the time they were 5, this encouraged those who matured sexually early to the detriment of the condition of the herds. The inheritance of an Arab tooth was also a disaster in this department even if it came with a pretty head. It was probably for this reason that the descendants of Denny Danny, who was probably descended from one of the Welsh stallions with Arab blood, were either grade I (the top grade) or grade 3 (unacceptable condition) in the filly premium scheme. All the other stallions recorded fillies middling to good or middling to poor. Early maturity was considered not to be present in stallions, as they were not required to be passed until they were 4 years old, they were known to grow till 7 years and not to be fully made up till 8 years. Another problem is that fillies who keep good condition will sometimes foal at 3 years; David Stagg's research found 13%, and this does the filly no favours.

In spite of Lascelles's reply the Ministry gave a grant for stallion premiums, taken over briefly by the War Office (predecessor of the Ministry of Defence), then by the Racecourse Betting Control Board and finally by the Betting Levy Board and administered by the National Pony Society. In 1990 the majority was still used for stallion premiums but a substantial amount to blood typing stallions and some to insurance against being run over. Blood typing in due course gave way to DNA testing. Unfortunately the grant ended for all but the rare breeds in 2000.

When most of England was enclosed for agriculture the office of Woods tried to enclose most of the Forest for timber growing. The deer destroyed trees and were no longer needed for winter meat, so the Deer Removal Act was passed in 1852 to get rid of them. Although the numbers were much reduced they fortunately failed to exterminate the deer. Lord Arthur Cecil considered this Act was another reason for the increase of scrub on Forest lawns. Scrub again increased enormously with the very small number of ponies turned out during World War 11. In 2005 the number of fallow deer is only half what it was 20 years ago whilst the number of red deer has considerably increased. The balance between the species of large herbivores needs careful monitoring.

The old four stallion idea of having a good imported stallion in-hand for the use of breeders was revived in 1918/19 when the polo pony stallion Field Marshall, a chestnut with three stockings and a blaze, was hired by the Lyndhurst Society; he stood 14.2hh and was by Marechal Niel by Rose Water, a very famous stallion in several pony stud books. His dam, Polo Queen, was out of a black Welsh mare. He certainly imparted quality but also a lot of white markings, inherited by his grandson Brookside Spitfire and Brookside David whose blaze extended over his eye, which was wall in consequence. By 1920 it

Old Beaulieu Rd sale 1960 (above) *and new sale yard, 2002.*

was decided outside blood should be confined to other Mountain and Moorland stallions so Field Marshall's place was taken for one season by the Fell Weardale Hero. One well known judge wondered if the progeny of these ponies would ever run out on the Forest and Commoners' opinion was that 'those with the most old Forest blood stayed out the longest' almost certainly because generations in the same place produced a tolerance to local parasites. This view prevailed and the Stud Book was closed to outside blood in 1935, Jester, a chestnut Dartmoor being the last outsider allowed. Brookside Judy, a descendant of Weardale Hero, and a well known show pony, ran out throughout World War II; her daughter Brookside Juliet, dam of the stallion Beacon Julian, and Julian ran for many years, Juliet being a particularly good doer perhaps because she did not foal till she was 6 but then had 14 foals.

PONY SALES

The charter for Ringwood's regular Wednesday market goes back to the Middle Ages and some ponies would always have been sold there; but the most important sale was Lyndhurst Fair, held on the first Thursday in August on Swan Green. Swan Green was also the site for the first few stallion shows. As motor traffic increased, the police considered the site obstructive and dangerous. At that time most ponies sold left the Forest by train, so a sale yard was built at Beaulieu Road opposite Lyndhurst Road station. With its earth-floored, wooden-railed pens, it was much safer for handling unhandled stock than the concrete-floored, steel-railed pens of cattle markets and in the eighty years of its existence no pony broke a leg there.

By the year 2000 it had been patched and patched and the people mingling with pushchairs in the passages down which the ponies were driven was no longer acceptable to Health and Safety. Building a new saleyard was very expensive so the Pony Society passed the running of the sales to a Livestock Committee with members from the Pony Society and the Commoners Defence Association, who were able to get funding through Forest Friendly Farming. Before cattle sales were so regulated some were held on the old site and whilst the original Lyndhurst Fair date has been kept more sales have been added. With the loss of most of the Avon valley farmers breeding ponies after World War I and the loss of back-up grazing due to enormous development in the area, most Commoners had to sell most of their foals. August was too soon to sell foals and there were too many for a single sale. A

September and October foal sale came in and during the height of the pony boom after World War II there were six late summer/autumn sales and a spring sale largely for unpassed colts and yearlings who had not been found before the last autumn sale. The Publicity Group's introduction of a Foal Show before the October sale and a Youngstock Show before the spring sale has encouraged new buyers, who felt they could not cope with an unhandled pony, as at least those in the show would be handled. Some Commoners are now halter-breaking their foals even when they are not entered in the show. The image of the sales has improved with the new yard. There is now a spring sale, and further ones in August, September, October and November. The December sale has been dropped; the stallion scheme has hopefully done away with late foals.

5
SHOWING AND RACING

ON AUGUST BANK HOLIDAY 1905 a show was held on Burley Lawn in conjunction with the Burley Athletes who ran a race from the Chapel to the show ring across Frogmoor: a course that would present difficulties today, wet feet and gorse scratched legs to start with. This show was a success and led to the first breed show that was held by the newly formed Burley & District New Forest Pony & Cattle Society, whose aim was to try, by offering prizes and premiums at a show, to improve Commoners' stock in the way the Lyndhurst Society for the Improvement of New Forest Ponies had been doing for 15 years with stallions. They also started a Stud Book, at first printing entries in the Annual Report. The definition of a New Forest pony was: 1. One known to the Agisters as such, or 2. One whose dam has run on the Forest for at least one season as a 3-year-old or upwards, and whose sire was a pony stallion passed by the Verderers or standing in the New Forest Parliamentary District.

The show was held on August Bank Holiday, then the first Monday in August, in Burley Manor Park. Unfortunately no documents seem to have survived for this show, but the catalogue for 1907 is available and classes would not be much different except that, on Lord Lucas's recommendation, the height for broodmares was increased to 13 hh from 12.3hh. In 1907 classes were held for mare with foal at foot: 22 entries for prizes £3, £2 and £1 with additionally three premiums offered by NPS and seven £1 premiums. A second brood mare class was for branded and tail marked mares who had run out through the previous winter without being hand fed and were owned by Commoners occupying not more than 20 acres, 6 entries. Classes for yearlings: 11 entries; 2-year-old-fillies and geldings (also 11 entries) and 3-year-old fillies (15 entries) in addition to prizes of £2, £1, 10/, 5/-; ten premiums of £1 were offered to be paid when the ponies were shown the following year to avoid immediate selling. In order to ensure the same pony came back the following year, premium winners were branded with the society brand under the mane, near side. The brand was a dot in a triangle.

There were classes for cows and heifers, all dairy type suitable to run the Forest, sows and donkeys, but the 2 donkey classes only attracted 5 entries. A prize for the best conditioned donkey, a match race, or a race once round the ring all failed to get many entries so were soon dropped, but there was a brief revival when the stallion show was moved to August Bank Holiday Saturday. For three years a donkey show was held on the Sunday afternoon.

Races were held round the perimeter of the park, about 5 furlongs for New Forest ponies not exceeding 12.2hh, 13hh and 13.2hh and an open race of 10 furlongs for ponies not exceeding 14.2hh the property of farmers residing in the New Forest parliamentary district. There were three jumping classes – New Forest, 14.2hh and horses; a water jump (the water was held in a tarpaulin) was included. There were harness classes for New Forest ponies not exceeding 12.2hh and over 12.2hh and for New Forest ponies suitable for draught in Forest Trucks, at least one of whom had her foal running loose beside her. There was a best ride and drive from among these entries; there was also a driving competition round markers at not less than 8 mph. There was an average of 10 entries per class. The day ended just after 7 pm (in

Pinhorn's Bicton Judy: 1907 brood mare winner.

Jessie Taylor Laddie 1910. Commoners Hack Class.

theory) with a potato race for New Forest ponies contested by 9 men and a girl! And a consolation 5 furlong race ridden bareback. The show did not start till 11 am but many exhibits had quite a walk to get there: they were ridden, driven or led. Mr Pinhorn, who won the first class with his mare and foal, lived at Bicton, near Fordingbridge.

A band played in the afternoon, there was a flower and veg show; halters, forage and hurdles could be purchased on the field. Cold lunches cost 2/-, tea in the society tent 6p. The beer tent also sold wine and spirits, hence the charge £2.8p for police. There also appears to have been a coconut shy! Rosettes, flags, string, etc, came to £9.1s. The tea tent made a profit of £6.5.3. And the gate £75.17.9 at 6p a time! A grandstand was erected. There was no charge for the ground.

By 1913 the show was well established as a great social occasion; there was dancing in the evening; the Burley Band played popular tunes in the afternoon; it was estimated 4,000 people came, with 118 carriages and a few cars to see 400 entries. Premiums were offered for foals, a class for mares exceeding 13hh was introduced, but this only attracted 7 entries, as opposed to 40 under 13hh and the judges were disappointed at the quality of the bigger ponies. The races were greatly extended to:

1. Five furlongs; New Forest ponies not exceeding 13hh to carry 11 stone 7lb; 7lb allowed for each full inch under 13hh. Prizes £4, £2 and £1: 16 entries.

2. Quarter mile New Forest ponies not exceeding 13hh catch weights over 11 stone; prizes £3, £2, £1: 16 entries.

3 Five furlongs open; not exceeding 14hh catch weights over 9 stone: 10 entries.

4. Quarter mile New Forest ponies not exceeding 13.2hh, catch weights over 12 stone; prizes £3, £2, £1: 10 entries.

5. Quarter mile New Forest ponies not exceeding 13.3hh, owners up, catch weights over 12 stone; £2, £1: 6 entries. Ted Burry on Burton Bluebell beat Lord Lucas on the Nun.

6.Ten furlong open not exceeding 14.2hh, catch weights over 9 stone, £5, £2, £1.

There was a New Forest ridden class for the first time with 24 entries, a child's hunter class, riders under 15. (The following year a special was offered for the best girl rider!) And a selling class for New Forest ponies not under 13.2hh or over 5 years shown under saddle to be sold

Ponies suitable for draught purposes to be shown in Forest trucks 1911(note the foal).

Mrs Mudie's Daisy harness class ponies ex 12.2hh, 1911.

for not more than £25 for which there were 8 entries. Small Commoners were redefined as 'Not occupying more than 5 acres'.

The show continued throughout the great war but the social side suffered; there is a report in 1915 of Belgian refugees fighting Thorney Hill gypsies in the beer tent. Dr Howard stopped these gypsies fighting in the beer tent by throwing a bucket of cold water over them. Foals in those days were seldom led and at least one found his way into the beer tent. There are few records for the 20s and 30s but the harness classes went down and the ridden classes up and a set of jumps was made. The course was always the same, all on the left rein with no change of direction. It started with an upright brush about 5 strides from the collecting ring, an arrangement ensuring a high proportion of entries got no further. Those who did met an in and out of another brush, followed by an upright of two white rails. These fences were joined by hurdles, round the top of the ring to a white gate and on to a red wall, left again across the middle to the triple bar; all jumps were about 2ft 6in and there would be two jump offs when the jumps would

A child's hunter class in the Park in 1936:1st, the future Lord Darling on Brookside Judy, for many years secretary of the Bath and West Show. 2nd, the future Lord Manners, who served as Official Verderer many years later. 3rd, Dawn Kirby (Mrs Cree's elder daughter). 4th, Rosemary Mangin on Pinkie, later a New Forest Society and Council member and judge. 5th Stephanie Mackworth Praed now Mrs Brooks, a Connemara judge who runs a trekking centre in Connemara and the Connemara Pony Club, riding Thomas. 6th Nancy Keymer née Tate, riding Rowhill Mystery: she has had lifelong involvement with New Forest ponies; grandchildren are keen polo players on New Forest ponies.

be raised. A gymkhana was also introduced taking place in the lower ring after the in-hand classes and the show ended with musical tyres in the main ring, always to Soupee's Light Cavalry overture to which most, but never all, the ponies kept time.

The show also continued through World War II, entries in the harness class picked up and a beginner's pony class was added, where the rider showed how quiet the pony was by sliding over its tail, crawling under it, standing up on its back or opening an umbrella while mounted, etc. Another class, which would not have been approved by Health and

Safety, was the utility race where the pony was driven, ridden and led from a bicycle. Only the bicycles suffered and of course it was the fastest harness change that won. An open ridden class was popular.

1949 was the last show before the influence of stud bred ponies became apparent, the division between large and small was still 12.3hh and numbers both of brood mares under 12.3hh and over 12.3hh was about equal. Petrol rationing was still in force, many spectators came on bicycles but there were no cars. Oakleys four cattle lorries picked up entries round the Forest and a few exhibitors with a ration for agricultural use had lorries but most still came on their own hooves. In 1949 the Society sub and show entry fees were still 2/6. i.e. 12½p. Prize money £3, £2, £1, i.e. 3rd prize was 8 times the entry fee. From then on various things were tried to help stem falling gates - fancy dress, cushion polo, broomstick polo; in coronation year, a pageant of the queens of England put on by the Pony Club, who also did a musical ride. One year, a pageant of Forest history was performed by the performance winners. The other big change was the change of date to the last instead of the first Monday in August. This resulted in a great improvement in the weather and a drop of 10% in the weather insurance. The old bank holiday was notoriously wet but since the change there has only been one real soaker.

Lionel Edwards's drawing of Burley Show 1913; a very wet day.

Canford Scrapbook 1949 with Janet Ellis, now Williams, who organises the Breed Show.

After 1950 the height division gradually increased and so did the traffic. Manor Park became too small, it did not have enough parking or willing helpers to put up rings and dig the holes for the horrible loos! So the Breed Show moved to New Park's permanent ground. The donkeys were dropped and pigs are long gone and the donkey races were killed when someone actually taught their donkey to run straight. There is no longer a gymkhana and the fun classes, bareback jumping, children doing tricks with their ponies, the utility race hardly met the health and safety requirements.

The show became a 3-day show, the cattle, now all beef, were judged on the holding instead of coming to the show, beef cattle seldom being halter broken! With the loss of the races, Commoners largely lost interest. The performance classes now dominate; it is a long time since there were 40 brood mares in a class!

As an example of the more relaxed attitude to showing in the '60s, one lady showing her pony in-hand at a small show was wearing a fashionably full, calf length brightly printed cotton skirt and flip-flop sandals. As she ran her pony out the flip-flops flew off and, unabashed, she finished the class barefoot. Riding the ponies could be embarrassing for judges: one well known hunter judge, having found his first choice a little sticky, closed his legs smartly on the 13.0hh mare he had pulled in 2nd; she had won the point-to-point several times and he found himself doing a very fast circuit of the large ring. Bringing her back, he said to the rider, 'too many oats and not enough exercise,' to which she replied, 'She never has oats and has been ridden seven miles to get here.' Even more embarrassing was the occasion when, thinking it unfair not to ride all entries, the judge on the pony placed last was thinking whether she should change the 3rd and 4th around and got bucked off.

Today the standard is much more level than it used to be: you seldom see a pony that is really below standard, but then it could be hard to find anything good to say of the tail-enders, though one charming lady judge beamed at the disappointed child at the end of the line and said, 'What a generous head your pony has.'

When the show was held at the beginning of August, it was often

Dolores, by Picket Hermit ex Griselda, 1912: eventually sold to Ted Burry.

Dainty IV, foaled 1910, ancestress of Brookside David.

very wet. Lionel Edwards drew a particularly wet one in 1912. The main ring was notorious for a step across the middle, the result of wartime ploughing. One large harness judge trying an exhibit, on crossing this step was shot high in the air and disappeared into the body of the cart with a loud bang as the old vehicle's seat broke. When a pageant showing the death of Rufus was performed, Rufus, having been picked up and put in the charcoal burner Purkis's cart, was violently evicted at the same spot; being a good actor he lay there and Purkis drove on unaware till the commentator said, 'I think you have lost something.' The Show used to end with Musical Tyres, till one year Don Stainer arrived equipped with a tyre on the back of his pony!

Many aspects of pure showing have improved but while nearly all today's ponies trot and canter very well few really walk and hardly any really lengthen and stretch when asked to gallop. The NPS, by introducing mixed M & M Ridden and WHP competitions with finals at prestigious shows and no age limit on the rider, gave the native ponies an enormous boost badly needed. Stallion performance, grading schemes and greater interest in jumping and dressage followed and has enlarged the market for excellent ponies that do not win show classes. However this has made the maintenance of true native pony type and action of even greater importance. It is not enough to say basic conformation and action are common to all ponies, there are important differences such as a native pony should be deeper, cover more ground and have more bone than other ponies of similar size and there are also differences in way of going.

Showing has changed enormously in the last fifty years. Fifty years ago the in-hand classes were supreme but no geldings were shown; stallions were seldom included; quite a few Commoners showed their ponies. Ridden classes were judged as miniature hunters, judged by a hunter judge who always rode the ponies, and expected them to enter really walking on a loose rein. There was no individual show. The pony had to really walk and gallop, the whole class was galloped together but the rein was seldom changed. Overbent ponies were right out and ponies were shown hunting fit, never fat. Only plain browbands and cavesson nosebands were admissable, flash nosebands, martingales and numnahs were not. A plain loose ring or eggbutt snaffle was usual for novices and a double or plain pelham for open classes, everything else was considered a schooling aid, not for the ring.

Now the ridden classes are the most popular and working hunter pony (WHP) classes have really taken off; dressage is a relative newcomer. Everything has become much more professional and serious, but less fun. It is no longer the social event it used to be with a band and dancing in the evening, not to mention the results published in *The Times* the following morning.

STUD BOOK

At first a register of ponies shown was printed at the end of the Annual Report. The Polo Pony Stud Book (later the NPS) admitted M&M ponies to Vol. 5 of their Stud Book. There were different sections for each district and the New Forest was defined as 'difficult to give the exact description but the best are 12.2 to 13.2hh if taken off the Forest at weaning and done well for their first two winters; ponies often make 14.0 to 14.1hh. They sometimes have an apparent lack of bone but what there is should be of the very best quality, the feet wide and well formed, they are often considered goose rumped but their hocks should be all that can be desired. In colour they range through every variety but dun is rare and there are few if any picbald, the flea bitten greys which are very common show strong traces of an Arab cross. The shoulders though not always what might be desired in point of depth are almost invariably fine and well laid. It is a great characteristic of the New Forest pony to be always gay and alert and though extremely good tempered and docile when fairly broken, they are quite indomitable till fairly cornered; the true Forester is never sulky.'

The first Stud Book was produced in 1910; the work proved too much for the Hon. Sec. Mr Coots, who complained the Commoners only sent in their applications at the very last minute. Some things never change. Mr Kershaw was appointed and paid a salary. This volume contained 118 stallions divided into stallions that had run the Forest and pony stallions standing in the New Forest Parliamentary district; 356 mares whose dams must have run the Forest for at least one season as three-year-olds or upwards and a few un-numbered geldings. The first President and Chairman of the Burley and District New Forest Pony and Cattle Society, Lord Lucas, speaking of cross breeding, was opposed to crossing with horses because of loss of 'pony character' but TB blood he put in a different category for 'there can be found Thoroughbreds with their full share of "pony character" and besides they are the cream of horse flesh and there never was any milk spoilt by the addition of a little more cream!' (How times change: semi-skimmed being now so popular, and no one likely to be fined for selling milk with less than 4% butter fat, 8% for Channel Island milk.)'I believe TB blood will improve any pony, though from consideration of hardiness it should not come in undiluted, the same applies to Arab.'

He found the faults of all M&M ponies to be the same when visiting the West Country to find new blood. He was very impressed with the stock of the Welsh stallion Dyoll Starlight but complained his stock were so sought after they were very expensive which showed the value of a Stud Book in establishing bloodlines. He bought four: Picket Pole Star, Picket Greyling, Picket North Star and Picket Starlight, who, when he had run the Forest for a year or two, managed to look more Forest than Welsh. He also acquired Picket Hermit, a docked bay cob by a TB Timothy, grandson of Hermit who won the Derby in a snowstorm beating the favourite The Dun on whom Lord Huntington had bet his entire fortune and as a result had to sell his stately home. Picket Hermit became very popular, because, in spite of his TB blood, his stock did very well on the Forest. Picket Hermit sired Dainty IV who, having won the Child's Working Hunter Class at the breed show 6 times, became the ancestress of Brookside David. Up to 1989 she had 1,492 descendants registered. David sired Oakley Jonathan and when blood typing was introduced for stallions, Newmarket pointed out that some of this line had a blood type previously only found in TBs. The TB was five generations back!

One of the entries in the second section of the first Stud Book for stallions was Tommy Dodd I, 13.0hh chestnut foaled 1896 by Yuresson out of an Exmoor mare by Katerfelto, known in the Polo Pony Stud Book as Cathephelta, which confuses computers. His descendants are still around.

Dyoll Starlight.

Only two volumes of the New Forest Stud Book were published because the Great War intervened; Mr Kershaw was called up, and an acting Hon. Sec. took over; all registrations were sent to the National Pony Society(NPS) who continued to register all New Forest Ponies till 1960; by then it took so long and was claimed to be too expensive so a local register was started. This was for ponies who ran the Forest and were only shown at the breed show, Forest Fed class or ran in the point-to-point. This record was not printed so no one could look up a pony's breeding, so in 1960 the first red Stud Book appeared and it has been published annually ever since.

The lapse of registration during the war and the lack of breeding supplied afterwards is particularly frustrating in the Mudeford ponies. Mudeford Bluebell, for instance, won show classes and races but has no registered descendants and neither has Dolores, a daughter of Griselda, whom Mr Burry bought from Miss Blackmoor although he kept ponies and registered many after the war: breeding sire as 'Forest Horse' and breeding mare as 'Forest mare'. Miss Jackson was one of the few who kept up registrations so it was lucky Mr Burry bought Brookside David from her.

Lord Lucas had thought 13.0hh the height to go for as smaller ponies

Mrs Adams's Peters Goldie, Forest Fed winner.

did not sell so well there being too much competition from the other small breeds and he did not think anything much bigger would live on the Forest. So for a while 13.0hh was the limit on brood mares at the show but stallions in section 2 could be up to 14.2hh so presently it became necessary to make 14.0hh the limit for all; this increased to 14.2hh in 1955 and is now 148cm. It was finally agreed all ponies should have a registered dam so for a few years an appendix for Forest bred and running the Forest was kept for those without registered dams but known to the Agisters and committee to be Forest. This closed in Vol. 12; appendix stallions were only accepted for one year in Vol. 8. Harmonization of Stud Books within the EC demanded that the definition of registered should be 'Tracing only to ponies already registered in the British New Forest Stud Book' so the appendix had to go along with the First Cross and part bred registers now kept separately. Piebald and skewbald ponies descended from Shetland or vanner ponies were banned in 1949; blue eyed creams in 1970 because of the increased likelihood of breeding these from pale chestnut and palomino ponies. These were no longer accepted as stallions after 1991 as these dilute colours bred together can produce albinos who do not survive.

In spite of their mixed ancestry the ponies were becoming more of a type due to the environmental influence of the dam having to have run the Forest.

Writing in 1910, the well known pony judge Rev. T. Dale wrote,

> New Forest ponies have always been something of racehorses. In 1880's there was a little grey mare who was never beaten. Her owner tried a TB cross, but declared the mare better. On one occasion he drove her three miles to the course where she won three races in succession, six heats in all, and drove her home afterwards. Her progeny by Heron by Maccaroni were fast but not as fast as her. The NF pony is ideal for small holders having the weight and power to move a considerable load and the activity not to take too long about it and sufficient action to do it in style. They also show considerable stamina and weight carrying ability under saddle
>
> Three things are necessary to establish a first class breed: time to blend the various strains of blood, in-breeding sufficient to fix a type both mental and physical and long years of careful selection of the best breeding stock and herein lies the value of a Stud Book. In the end no general improvement will be made without Commoners culling sub standard mares.

Perhaps the above provided the inspiration for the 1911 innovation: the non hand-fed class for mares that lived continually on the Forest without extra winter feed. The owners had to be prepared to find

Forest Fed winner 1950s.

G.H. Morgan and the Nun, as a yearling, in 1909.

them, with the Agisters acting as 'beaters' to drive the mares towards the judges, who were impressed by the sight of the mares going across the rough ground. Lady Lucas brought the picnic hamper out by car and a good time was had by all. The following year the mares were judged in early spring, and condition was reckoned good considering the prolonged drought of 1911. The ponies moved with freedom and style, the best conditioned had the best conformation and the best yearling and 2-year-old were products of a 26 year-old-mare.

THE POINT TO POINT

The other innovation was the point-to-point; it may have been a revival as there is an old tradition of cross-country racing. Races had been held at Lyndhurst for years; stallions had often done well at them and of course sprint races were held at Burley Show, where Lionel Edwards drew them in 1912. From his drawings it certainly looks as if the ponies are living up to their reputation of carrying a stone a hand. The new race was held on Boxing Day 1911 over a 'take your own line' only disclosed at the meeting place, Bolderwood. Rain fell in torrents and the ground from Millyford Bridge to Ocknell Pond was very rough in places. Of 16 entries, 12 ran, the minimum weight was 11stone with

7lb added for each inch over 13.0hh, no allowance for shoes. The top weight over 3½ miles was 13 stone. The entries were:

name of pony	name of jockey	hh	weight carried
The Nun.	Lord Lucas	13.2hh	12st 7lb.
Burton Bluebell.	E. Burry.	13.3hh	12st 7lb.
Sopley Bluebell.	R.Phillpots	13.1hh	11st 7lbs.
Harrow Tommy (owner T. Stovold).	H. Forward	12.2¾hh	11st
East Boldre Lassie.	A. Evemy.	13.2hh	12st
Spion Kop.	Major Loudon.	13.2hh	12st
Duster. H. Watts.	J. Street.	12.2hh	11st
Purewell Rufus. (G. Lander)	J. Deer.	13hh	11st
Picket Black Beauty.	P. Kershaw.	13.3hh	13st

In future races ponies under 13hh were allowed a weight allowance of 7lb an inch under the maximum height.

Duster and Rufus fell in deep ground in Puckpits, being the only two to attempt the enclosure. The Nun fell on good ground and Burton Bluebell fell over her, nevertheless they finished 1st and 2nd; Sopley Bluebell was 3rd and Harrow Tommy 4th. Prizes £5,£3,£2 with similar prizes for the first three Small Commoners home. No entry fee.

Next year was even wetter. Sixteen runners met at Blackwater Bridge; much of the course from the NE corner of Poundhill enclosure to Sethorns Cottage was completely under water. Most entries ran together till joined at the Rifle Butts by Beaulieu King who had come another way; about a mile from the finish Harrow Tommy and Carmelite fell and Purewell Rufus and Burton Bluebell took the lead from the Nun, Rufus winning by a length. Subsequently two matches were run: the first had C. Evemy riding the Nun , W. Evemy on Burley Nigger, each accompanied by a pacemaker to decide the best course to have taken, but the Nun fell so the argument continued. The second over a flagged course from Ocknell Pond to Picket Post, owners up on the same ponies, was run at a great pace. The Nun won by 6 lengths. It needs to be remembered Lord Lucas had only one leg!

The third race had the first fine day. Seventeen entries met at The Queen's Head, Burley, at noon! They were taken to a point near the railway on Cranesmoor and finished at the top of Markway Hill; all went the same way, till some went up the side of the Brockenhurst road, which was too far to the right. Burton Bluebell won from Purewell

Scurry race at Burley Show in the 1950s..

Rufus with J. Bradford's Saltpeter 3rd.

In the years 1914-1918 there were no races. In 1919 the winner was F. Shutler on Starlight; in 1920 and 1921 W. Burry won, beaten the following year by Major Grovenor's Arch. Mr Burry got his revenge the next year.

Sopley Bluebell was a versatile pony, winning the 1910 Forest Trucks Class at Burley Show, in 1911 being Highly Commended as Commoners Hack and 2nd in the Scurry Race at Burley, as well 3rd in the point-to-point. In 1912 she was 2nd at the New Forest Pony Romsey Show, 3rd in the jumping, Highly Commended in the Forest Trucks, 2nd in the Child's Hunter and 2nd in the scurry, all at Burley Show.

Burton Bluebell later won the brood mare class at the NPS as well as at Burley.

After a gap in the records, we find in 1935 the first lady riders were recorded. There were three races, Open NF, Small Commoners and

Children; they ran together, starting at Picket Post and finishing at the junction of the Broomy Lodge Moyles Court roads. Riders were expected to go Marrowbones Hill, Pinnock, Roe Cottage, but it was again very wet so they preferred to stay on the dry ground to Handy Cross and cut down across Buckherd Bottom, consequently they came through the finish the opposite way from that expected. The finish could not have been more exciting. Mrs Kirby(later Mrs Cree) riding Bunny rode neck and neck with Ted Burry on Mudeford Nigger for the last half mile, Mrs Kirby just winning, close behind Miss Passy on Daphne dead heated with Miss Duckett on Beaver for 3rd. Starting ten minutes later, Miss E. Powell, riding A.Thomas's Juno, won the Small Commoners while J. Sparks on Laddie was first of five children home.

In 1936 a triangular course from Wilverley Post to Puckles Bridge and back was tried, 3 ½ miles as ridden, this time the Children went with the Open, and the Small Commoners on their own. The Open was won by R. Pultney with Summertime, the Small Commoners by R. Hayward on Zephyr (50 years later he won the Veterans on another Zephyr), while P. Mansbridge on Muss took the Children's from H.

Competitors for the New Forest point-to-point in the 1930s; Rachel Pultney in the centre.

Point to point.

Andrews's stallion Telegraph Rocketer. The spectators liked seeing the start and finish but it was not popular with competitors.

STALLION SHOW

The Stallion Show started in 1891 on a Saturday afternoon in April on Swan Green. Increased traffic caused it to move to Cuffnells Park, Lyndhurst, where the agricultural show was held. Only in-hand Forest running stallions were competing for some twenty premiums offered first by the Ministry of Agriculture then the Horse Race Betting Levy Board, divided by height at 12.3hh; there were some 30 entries in each class. These had first been inspected by the Verderers who considered about 80 stallions were necessary to cover the area. The youngstock had a separate ring and their premiums were not paid until they had run out from May 1st to August 1st as four-year-olds. Increased traffic moved the show to Cuffnells, Lyndhurst, where the agricultural show was held at the time. When Cuffnells was no longer available, the stallion show moved first to Sway, then to Holmsley and finally to Burley Manor Park on the Saturday before the Breed Show. The Bank Holiday was now the last, not the first weekend in August. Sunday was given over to a donkey show. The move from April to August in 1968 was because it was felt unfair to judge stallions who had wintered on the Forest against those who had been kept in and perhaps ridden; also to turn out fit stallions to chase mares who were very close to foaling was a bad idea, it also led to more road accidents. This problem had happened before. In the 1930s different premiums were given for corn- and non-corn-fed ponies and to avoid the corn-fed stallions chasing the mares, they were not allowed out till June 1st, by which time the herds were established and these ponies were considered interlopers and were chased off by the non-corn-fed; frustrated, they jumped into fields with riding pony mares, which was not popular and sometimes led to the stallion damaging himself on the fence. Turning them all out on the evening of the show again became the practice. Ridden classes for Forest run stallions had been introduced while Cuffnells was still the venue; gradually Stud Classes were added.

During the 1920s the Lyndhurst Society regretted the lack of support at the stallion show of Small Commoners. Rev. Dale reporting on the 1921 stallions:

> 1st Laby Loo by Sandy II, son and grandson of previous winners; brown pony of great bone and substance and plenty of stallion and pony character with some good stock to his credit, he moves well with level free action.
>
> 2nd Bayardo, own brother to above, previous premium winner, hardly as much power but more quality than his brother, a little short in his back ribs, Laby Loo's additional bone and substance make him more suitable for the Forest.
>
> 3rd Tam O'Shanter, a very good pony, his sire Loch Corrie has left some excellent stock and Tam's stock have a good reputation, he has good pony character, remarkably short cannons and great depth through the heart[ancestor of Knightwood Spitfire].
>
> 4th Purewell Jumbo by Gorley Pride, a previous winner who has sadly left the Forest having left good stock. Jumbo is a nice pony of good quality and few Forest faults, he moves fairly well.
>
> 5th Holmsley Taffy by Sandy II, a compact pony on short legs but short in the neck.
>
> 6th Godshill Georgie, a capital 13.2hh pony with fair action and great pony character.

Pony character and progeny feature largely in all Rev. Dale's judgements.

Although other activities had stopped during the Great War, the shows went on.

The councils of the two societies changed very slowly, most members staying till they died. Mr Stovold was secretary of the Lyndhurst Society for 30 years. Times were hard in the '30s so the subscription was reduced to 2/6 and remained at that till after the next war. A report in a London paper of poor ponies in the Forest was hotly disputed in the Verderers' Court. Mr Alway, representing both the Pony Societies and the Commoners' Defence, said, 'Any deterioration in the ponies condition was due to lack of drainage, there were only half the number of ponies depastured as in 1890 and £300 spent on Holmsley Bog would recover over 600 acres of pasture.' This argument continues: the situation has deteriorated still further: in 2004 discussion on this site for three hours in pouring rain achieved nothing.

A stallion in-hand scheme started in 1935 when the stallion show winner **Orchard Pershore** (chestnut) was chosen to run in old Park Ground, Brockenhurst, with 25 approved mares. Premiums were given to his foals at the 1936 show but not paid till they came again as

Miss P V Mangin on Busy Lizzy 1993

Lionel Edwards's depiction of Burley Show races 1913.

yearlings. This scheme fell victim to World War II but was revived in 1947 when Newtown Spark ran in Vereley, it ran for several years till it became impossible to find anywhere suitable to run the stallion, it was also considered that the private studs provided enough opportunity for mares to visit.

The non-hand fed class started again in 1945 and has been held ever since but is now called the Forest Fed class. Stallions judged partly on progeny seen was added but when stallions no longer ran all year this was reduced to a premium for the stallion with the best foals.

In the 1930s Rhinefield Polo Club, trying to make polo available to a wider, less well-off membership, had a rule that no pony could be played that had cost more than £85; this offered a new market for Forest ponies, who took kindly to the game. The Pony Club also provided a good market. Mr Burry suggested a class for Children's ponies of value not exceeding £25. The winner could be claimed at that price and was. It attracted a large entry.

In 1937 there were only three people who were not members of both societies, many council members and officials were common to both, so it was agreed to amalgamate them and in 1938 the New Forest Pony Breeding & Cattle Society came into being, with Sir Berkeley Pigott as Hon. Sec. and Sir George Meyrick as Chairman. The new Society was offered 16 acres at Stocks Farm, Burley, as a permanent show ground,

2003 point-to-point.

site for stallion in-hand and winter keep. However Sir George said he had received many letters both for and against but he felt that the ground could be rather wet and it was unwise for the Society to lock up all of its funds. This view was carried unanimously – how wrong they were. In its next breath the council pointed out that stallions kept by the Avon valley farmers were no longer available and Commoners would need more help with winter keep; the following year no field could be found for the stallion in-hand.

The NPS show was held in the grand hall, Islington, in March 1939; a train came up from the West Country picking up ponies along the way; they were led through London by a mounted policeman. The Society agreed to pay half the cost of travel – 16/11 per pony (under £1). Ten went; they were judged with the Exmoors and three ponies from Burley; Miss Jackson's Brookside Judy, ridden by Olga Golby, Miss Richard's Jason Weller and Miss Clayton's Pretty Polly, a rather leggy bay mare with large round ears like Micky Mouse but a good ride, were 1st, 2nd and 3rd in the ridden class. The previous year (1938),16 had been entered in the ridden class for NF, Dartmoor and Exmoor. Miss A. McGrath had won with Minstead Gay Girl, Brookside Judy was 4th. The Royal was held at Windsor and put on a ridden NF and Exmoor class, won by Brookside Judy from Miss Jackson's other entry, Brookside Tommy Tucker was 2nd. Show ponies did not have it so easy in those days. Judy was ridden from Burley to Romsey and back to add to her winnings. Miss McGrath is still showing New Forest ponies in 2005; what loyalty to the breed.

RACES

Lyndhurst Racecourse survives in name only; it appears to have had its heyday in the 18th century, since the races were revived on September 23rd, 1858, after a lapse of more than ten years. There are hints of races held on St Stephen's day (Boxing Day) that were stopped by the Puritans. Balmer Lawn took over from Lyndhurst between 1882 and 1905. In 1882 the Deputy Surveyor, Lascelles, made an application to his boss, the Commissioner for Woods, for permission to hold Annual Races at Balmer Lawn and to erect a stand for spectators saying, 'The races are restricted to New Forest ponies and therefore good for the breed.' The residents of Brockenhurst protested at the number of tourists attracted, particularly bicyclists! The date was moved from August Bank Holiday, then the first Monday in August, to the last Monday. With two refreshment booths, the Verderers objected to the booths and holes dug to fence the run in but not to the races. Their real objection was to the Deputy Surveyor giving permission without consulting them. First Prize for the 12.3hh and under race was £5, the entry fee being 1/-; today's point-to-point first prize is still £5 but the entry fee is £2 (1/- = 5p). Ponies of 13.2 hh had a £10 first prize at a time when an agricultural worker's wage was £5 a month.

The point-to-point has been run across the Forest every Boxing Day since 1911 except during the two World Wars, and sprints were held round Burley Manor Park in conjunction with the Breed Show from 1906, however the high time for New Forest pony racing was the 1960s when the Young Farmers held Annual Races at New Park Buckhound field; regular meetings were held at Matchams and on the playing field at Bransgore plus odd ones and midnight steeplechases round about. Whenever the Commoners had cause for celebration it was invariably extra races. Health and Safety would be appalled by most of these but few jockeys or ponies came to any harm and they were enormous fun.

The Boxing Day point-to-point is held in a different part of the Forest every year. Competitors are only informed of the meeting place the afternoon before and may be taken up to two miles to the start from there. They then pick their own line to the finish whose approximate position has been advertised. Most races are over 3 miles but Children and Veterans only 1½ miles. The ponies are handicapped by height, 14.2hh carry a minimum of 11st 7lb; 7lb being allowed for each full inch under the maximum, many carry quite a bit overweight, and some go much further than 3 miles! The course builder tries to choose a course with several different routes. Do you go through the enclosure, shorter but two gates; will your pony jump gates? Do you go over the hill or round - flatter but heavier going? If you go what you think is the shorter way, will your pony go as fast as if he had company; how fast are the others going? These decisions are talked of long afterwards. The event draws a large crowd, although they can only see the last few hundred yards. The real problem with this popularity is parking for all the cars and lorries which restricts where it can be held.

Post War racing

The point-to-point held on Christmas Eve 1946 from the railway east of Matley Wood to Boltons Bench was only 2½ miles. The open NF race was won by Miss R. Mangin's Bob, the Small Commoners by R. Ings's Myrtle and the Children's by P. Mansbridge on Brown Jack. The following year the races reverted to the traditional date and distance. Since then, except when postponed for frost or once till Easter because of foot and mouth restrictions, this has remained the format. Sometimes the start has been somewhat delayed to allow the frost to thaw; once there was some snow on the ground and on two occasions competitors came through the finish from opposite directions. Gamesmanship has always played a part, as when someone known to be familiar with the route was followed by everyone else but as his pony did not really stay the distance, he led them all through a bog where passing was not possible, which allowed him to sprint to the finish, his race finishing after what should have been the following one.

A race for colt-hunting ponies not exceeding 15.0hh, for which the Agister verified the pony had been on four drifts, was soon added, ponies could also qualify by hunting with either pack of NF Hounds. Following complaints from lady riders that they had to carry too much weight in this race, a Lady's Race was added; also a Novice NF; whilst the Children's Race was divided into 10-13 year age group and 14-16 years. The next addition was a Novice Children's and a Veterans' run together but with an NF Section and an Open Section. More recently a Heavy Weight Race for horses that have been colt hunted, carrying a minimum of 15 stone has been added; the latest, rather controversial idea, is a medium weight no height limit colt hunters. As there are now very few opportunities for ponies to lose their novice status, the Novice Children's Race has been dropped and the Open NF and Small Commoners are frequently run together. Small Commoners were changed to Young Commoners in 1905 but did not get filled. These races have become so popular and draw such a crowd that it has become difficult to find different areas to run them where it is possible to park the spectators' cars and to find a meeting place where all the competitors lorries and trailers can be accommodated. Health and safety also requires stewards on the course and at the finish.

6
WORLD WAR II & AFTER

SEVERAL FORESTERS DISTINGUISHED THEMSELVES in a 100-mile ride organised by *Country Life* in 1939 but the year ended with war and blackout and a three-fold rise in road accidents on the Forest. Three members offered keep to protect some and many were taken off, large areas of Forest were commandeered and the number turned out went down to 900, with a great increase of scrub invading lawns; the area complained of by Mr Always carried 40 head of milking cows plus several ponies through the war.

Now there are never more than about ten ponies and a few cattle! Miss Jackson's book has the sad entry, 'no shows, Judy turned to Forest'. She bred several foals.

The ponies contributed to the war effort by supplying blood for making anti-tetanus vaccines, as blood could no longer be imported from Holland. Three hundred and forty-nine mares were rounded up for this purpose, the owners being paid 15/- each. Three hundredweight of papers and old Stud Books were sent for salvage and considered to have provided enough pulp for a single sheet Annual Report. The Stallion Show and Breed Shows were held throughout the war. **Bettesthorne Caesar** and **Minstead Rex** took the stallion show honours. At the 1941 breed show an open Hack Class attracted 45 entries, every sort of cart came and hundreds of bicycles but not a single car! Sir Berkeley kept things going, being Hon. Sec. of the Pony Society, the Commoners Defence, the Polo Club and District Commissioner of the Pony Club.

The non-hand-fed class started again in 1945; a Stallion Class judged partly on progeny was added later. The point-to-point was held on Christmas Eve 1946 but this was not popular and the following year it reverted to Boxing Day. The Stallion in hand re-started in 1946, Newton Spark running in Vereley for three years. Special premiums were given to his foals at the show. Brookside Spitfire ran on the other side of the drive in the third year, but jumped over and fought Spark and so was returned to the Forest. Denny Danny ran at the grove in 1950 but soon after the rise of the private studs made the scheme redundant.

The first post-war show drew a record entry and a record gate. H. Peckham's Dolly won the open and Small Commoner's brood mare classes, all 12.0hh of her! Miss O. Burry's Dolly Grey IX by Brookside Firelight ex-Dolly, a grey race pony bought from the Forest Gypsies won the ridden championship. Firelight was rejected as overheight as a four-year-old. The height limit was not raised for some years; then it was still 14.0hh. He went on to win as a cob but as a three-year-old sired two champion stallions – Newtown Spark and Brookside David as well as a champion mare in Dolly Grey. At the 1949 show no pony exceeded 13.3hh and the division between large and small was 12.3hh; there were as many small as large ponies.

EXPORT

The immediate post-war generation of children were pony mad, they had no computers, few televisions but far more freedom; there was little traffic, petrol was rationed, and not many mothers worked full time. This meant they were available to escort children to Pony Club and help when they got there. They also ran many small gymkhanas, hunter trials, etc. Children hung around wherever there were ponies, getting free rides in exchange for helping, some even preferred helping to riding; parents were bombarded with pleas for a pony.

Meanwhile Europe was hungry, the meat market put a floor on prices and young stock prices compared well with cattle so numbers soared, augmented by bought-in ponies turned out to breed with little regard to quality or adaptability. There had always been some 'lane creepers', who followed the road verges off the Forest, but as numbers increased as did traffic, so did road accidents, ponies were rounded up and their owners fined. The Continent was recovering and also had pony-mad children and the advantages of starting to ride on a pony, instead of a large horse, were acknowledged. Britain had ponies, so the export boom began. First it was for the 'lane creepers', who were larger and fatter. Then pedigrees were in demand, as they were by the private studs, but many registrations were just 'Forest horse, Forest mare'; this was acceptable as for a long time the Verderers had only passed registered stallions so even if it was not known which stallion had covered which mare it had to have been a registered pony. 'Forest mare' was a pony that ran all her life on the open Forest and was known to the Agister and members of the Registration committee to be pure bred.

Mrs Spooner got the minimum value below which a pony could not be exported through Parliament to stop the live meat export trade in 1957. A great many of the best ponies were sold abroad and too many of the less well adapted ponies bred from and so there was a problem with poor ponies on the Forest in the early spring; the ponies in general got an undeservedly bad name, and very poor youngstock prices at the sales. Although neglect encouraged the survival of the fittest, because man had removed the predators, who would have quickly dealt with the unfit, some less hardy were surviving (just). Gradually with tougher stallion assessment, condition inspections and the pressure of market forces, things improved. As the importing countries bred their own ponies, the export market died back till only the best and outcross bloodlines could be sold. Export brought us into contact with Continental breeding methods, particularly the idea that only ponies that had proved themselves capable of doing what their progeny were required to do should be bred from. So stallions started competing to prove themselves.

The first recorded export of a Forest pony was in 1911 when Burton Sligo went to Australia, unfortunately there is no record of where or to whom he went. The most exotic export was a 12.2 hh black mare, who had to have no white spots in her mouth; she went as a child's pony, along with a household cavalry horse, as a diplomatic present to the King of Nepal.

Burton Starlight and Burton Sligo.

Virginia II at North Falmouth, Massachusetts, with her owner Monica Dickens and daughters Pamela and Prudence.

The first post-war exports were to Holland and proved very successful children's ponies, so they soon started breeding their own in large numbers, going for a large light quality type. The first two ponies to go to Denmark were taken by an English lady who settled there with her family and two llamas; these soon attracted attention as they kept escaping. The ponies were much admired and taught many children to ride in spite of the fact that their owner never learnt to speak Danish. Exports began to boom and daughter societies were set up in all the Scandinavian countries, Belgium, Holland, France and Germany; a few ponies also went to Austria, Spain, Italy and Switzerland. The Society sent ponies to Equitana horse fair in Germany on three occasions. Initially there were a few problems with papers due to language difficulties; one pony in the first Dutch Stud Book had the pedigree and description of a pony we registered in 1910! Dealers took loads of ponies and buyers who had first pick of the ponies had first pick of the papers and chose those with the longest pedigrees irrespective of whether the description matched the pony they had. These blips were fairly soon sorted, unlike the Golden Wonder problem that soured relations between the relevant societies for some years.

Brookley Katrine, four-year-old mare presented by the Society to HM The King of Nepal. The pony had to be free of black spots in its mouth.

Furzey Lodge Golden Wonder, a chestnut two-year-old colt, was not considered anything very special, so it was rather a surprise when he was bought to go to Holland as a stallion. That November it was considered even more surprising when he won the pre stallion passing (the Dutch have a preliminary inspection of colts in the autumn and the proper passing in the spring) and glowing reports were received. The following February a party from the Forest were invited to see the stallion passing. Golden Wonder, looking superb and moving very well, won against strong opposition, but close inspection raised doubts that this was the pony sold. He appeared to have grown a lot, his white heel had changed sides, he had a very fine coat with a bronze sheen, he was remembered as a much yellower chestnut, and above all there was no trace of a brand. His breeder confirmed he had been branded; it is against the Verderers' by-laws to turn out an unbranded pony, and he had run out. The Dutch were informed of the suspicions, but were so delighted with the pony they did not want to know and he proved a very popular stallion. Some years later his mother was sold for export; by then blood typing was available and this showed she was most unlikely to be Golden Wonder's dam. By then he had covered many mares sent to him in good faith, excuses were found not to pass colts by him as stallions, he disappeared and after many meetings it was reluctantly agreed to allow the registration of foals with no more that 6½ % of his blood.

Møelherons Tajo was a most successful pony stallion in Europe. He won several gold medals himself in international pony dressage teams. He stood in Germany but was bred in Denmark by Peveril Probus out of a Forest bred mare, both imported from the UK.

Apart from Europe, ponies were exported to North America: in 1951 Nancy's Fancy, bred by W. House by Bettesthorne Caesar, who was six generations descended from Burton Sligo, who had been exported to Australia. Nancy Deeds also sent Beacon Perdita ex-Bettesthorne Kate whose dam was Bettesthorne Caesar's sister. Perdita had won the Mare Championship at the Breed Show and the ridden class at Romsey as a three-year-old. She went up to Glasgow by train, travelling loose as the headcollars the railway provided were designed for Shires! She was then shipped to New York with three TB yearlings from Ireland. It was some time before others followed but Mrs Holbrook became an enthusiast in Canada starting with the stallion Mudeford Streak and a few enthusiasts have continued to support the breed in both USA and Canada.

A few ponies were also sent to Australia before transport costs became prohibitive. The breeding of ponies here where numbers are so limited has probably been saved by the option of importing frozen semen, which is now possible from several stallions.

7
1950s ONWARDS

AT THE SAME TIME AS THE CLAUSE that dams of registered ponies must have run on the Forest was removed in 1949, piebald and skewbald ponies were barred and the Verderers persuaded to allow only fully registered ponies to be passed as stallions. The 1950s saw the perimeter of the Forest fenced along the main roads; luckily this coincided with the export boom, so that there was a market for the lane creepers; but then many were bred overseas, transport costs increased enormously and an outbreak of metritis in Thoroughbreds made many countries insist on expensive testing for all imported stock, so the boom ended and the average price of foals at the sales fell by 7% at a time of high inflation.

For several years a team jumping competition was held alternately in Holland and the Forest.

Veterinary certificates of freedom from hereditary unsoundness became compulsory for stallions in 1970 when the Ministry passed stallion licensing to the breed Societies who in due course added a few more conditions to the original Ministry list. An inspection at two years, with blood typing, came in in 1970 and a further inspection, particularly to check height and parrot mouth, at five years was added. In 1968 the stallion show moved to August.

1960 saw the first ridden class at the stallion show, at first confined to stallions that ran out on the Forest. It was also the year the first Red Stud Book was published. The NPS had become very slow in processing registrations, published the Stud Book at very long irregular intervals and was expensive.

A Supreme Championship cup to commemorate Mr Burry's famous mare **Dolly Grey** was presented for the first time at the 1957 Breed Show but the races had to be dropped as less of the park was available and more was required for parking the ever increasing number of lorries and trailers. It became more difficult to get voluntary helpers and there was inadequate water so the show was moved to New Park, Brockenhurst.

DOLLY GREY IX 7767 NPS

Foaled: 1942
Sire: Brookside Firelight
Dam: Mudeford Dolly, Champion
Owner and Breeder: Miss O. Burry, Balmer Lawn, Brockenhurst
1947 Grey Mist IV, f, by Brookside David, Champion
    Bred 1953 Early Mist, c, by Gorley and 2 cross breeds
1951 Golden Victory, c, by Moorbridge Victory, premium winner
1954 (colt drowned) by Denny Danny
1955 Meld, f, by Denny Danny, winner
    Bred 1958 Happy Medoly, f, by Duikers Happy & Glorious, winner
        Bred 1966 Pykle Picador, by Burton Starlight, premium winner
    1960 Little Tina, f, by Mudeford Grey Ranger, winner, exported to Sweden
    1962 Happy Memory of Ramblers, c, by Duikers Happy & Glorious
    1964 Happy Danny, c, by Duikers Happy & Glorious
    1965 Happy Monarch, c, by Duikers Happy & Glorious
    1967 Glorify. c, by Duikers Happy & Glorious
1956 Grey Magic, f, by David Gray, Champion
    Bred 1961 Gray Diamond, f, by Mudeford Peter
        Bred 1965 Grey Star, c, by Burton Starlight
        Bred 1966 Glitteriing Star, f, by Burton Starlight
        Bred 1967 Glitter, f, by Burton Starlight
    1962 Grey Friars, c, by Mudeford Peter, Exported to Holland
    1963 Magic Diamond, f, by Mudeford Peter
        Bred 1967 Plunder, c, by Merrie Marauder
    1965 Summer Magic, c, by Deeracres Summertime
1957 Blue Orchid, f, by Dated Piece, GSB winner show jumping
1958 Broken Doll, f, by Dated Piece, GSB winner show jumping
1959 Dorian Grey, c, David Gray, Champion
1960 St David, c, by David Gray, winner
1962 Royal Crusader, c, by Duikers Happy & Glorious, exported to Holland. Retired to be herd lead mare

A performance pony competition, judged on points so that ponies could compete from all round the country, started in 1973. The first winner appropriately was Mrs Green's Priory Pink Petticoats; the prizes were presented at Olympia Christmas Show for the first four years. The year Frank of Crabbswood won, the winning ponies performed a Forest pageant, Frank ably representing the Forest Scouts. Other scenes included the death of Rufus, smuggling, etc. The following year a diminutive Puckpits Maid Marion, ridden by Richard Pritchard, won and a versatile competition, including a small cross-country course with an attractive water hazard, was filmed by TVS for its programme 'Out of Town'. Winners included Deeracres Franco, who won the Out of Town cup for best harness pony and distinguished himself by trying to get back into his trailer while still attached to his cart!

During the 1980s when Commoning was very unprofitable it was thought Commoners would probably keep mature mares who were regular breeders and good enough doers not to require extra winter feeding and so were cheap to keep and maintain the Commoning way of life; but youngstock, who gave no return in the form of foals for sale for four years, and often needed extra feeding while growing and teething, would be sold. A filly premium scheme to encourage the keeping of good fillies was devised. Fillies were graded on condition in the early spring and those who achieved a reasonable grade and were considered to have reasonably good conformation were awarded a premium. Over the years the age crept up and eventually premiums were extended to unregistered ponies; this meant information just beginning to emerge on bloodlines that kept condition was no longer collated and nothing was being done to improve quality. After six years, when the number of ponies on the Forest had risen too high for both the Forest and the market, the scheme was dropped.

Dolly Grey IX led by Ted Burry.

Mrs Harvey Richards presenting Performance Pony Awards, 1978: (left
to right) *1st Rupert, bred on Forest; 2nd Puckpits Maids Marion (ridden
by Richard Pritchard); 3rd Furzey Lodge Autumn Amber (ridden by Miss
Burtenshaw); 4th Staplecross Summer Holiday (ridden by Miss Horsefield);
5th Burton France; 6th Beacon Starflight (ridden by Lucy Stiles).*

The formation of the New Forest Pony Enthusiasts Club, a BHS
Riding Club using only NF ponies, was founded in 1985. In May 1989
it put on a most professional Musical Ride for 12 stallions who spent
a week at the Food and Farming Exhibition in Hyde Park. One night
a small black NF stallion was swapped with one of the Household
Cavalry's horses. Over several years this musical ride performed
all over the country: 35 different stallions took part, often travelling
together and being tied side by side along the lorry. They behaved
like perfect gentlemen, even if at one rehearsal in a covered school
one stallion tried to fight himself in the mirror. A quadrille consisting
of one mare, one gelding and two stallions doing a Morris Dance with
clashing sticks and bells on their fetlocks and an enormous number of
roses in manes and tails, was third at Olympia. The enthusiasts have
had an excellent record at the Riding Club finals, winning the Prix
Caprille Championship in 1990 and also qualifying for the dressage
finals at Malvern. Club teams have done consistently well in both
dressage and jumping.

The Pony Society introduced stallion testing in the 1950s with an aptitude test with the walk timed, the idea being to test willingness to work alone and test the pony's natural paces and obedience, not his level of schooling; a jumping course, again judged on the pony's attitude and shape over the jumps, not just on clear rounds; and a stamina test, eight miles in an hour in groups of six, including a gallop, passing the free running ponies, behaving in company, opening gates, going through water and galloping together. There was also a progeny inspection and those whose progeny were considered up to standard were printed in the Stud Book.

GRADING

In order to provide more information for breeders and buyers, a grading scheme was introduced for Forest running mares, who had bred a foal, could be inspected for conformation, action and type and achieve a basic grade, extended the next year to stud mares. Level one on the mare herself; level two if three of her progeny have achieved certain criteria and level three if both the mare and her progeny qualify on performance. When they had had three foals that had achieved performance or showing winnings, they could apply to become silver

Ms Andree's Peveril Peterborough, Mrs M. Bryan's Dewlands Val Doonican, Merrie Stud's Merrie Marmalade.

Mrs Harry Richards presenting the prizes at the President's Challenge to Fiona Biddle on Peveril Peterborough partnering John Whitaker.

graded and if they themselves had similar achievements they could become gold graded. Performance grading for jumping and dressage was also introduced. The grade depended on the height of the jumps and the standard of dressage test taken. With jumping the height of the pony is also a factor.

An elite scheme is also in place with marks for placings at various shows and competitions going both to the pony and its parents. At the moment it is rather too show-orientated but hopefully this can be improved. The outstanding stallion on progeny is Peveril Peter Piper and on performance Peveril Peterborough and Wayland Cranberry.

Stallions to run the Forest have long been inspected by the Verderers for conformation, action and type as well as having to be vetted at two and five years but stud stallions only needed vetting. In 2002 it was decided that all stallions should be inspected at two years old.

The Forest running stallion scheme, whilst undoubtedly successful in the short term, is not sustainable for long as too many genes would be lost. The higher standard of passing must be kept but the percentage of stallions to mares will have to increase The next step should be a similar standard applied to the mares but this has to be voluntary and so is unlikely. It is hoped grading mares to the approved standard will show the way and increased premiums for graded mares and improved prices for their foals would help. At the start of the stallion scheme the number of mares was reduced but has since increased again, which is a pity. The stallion scheme successfully reeduced the number of foals in the first two years, but the ponies adapted by leaving thier haunts to find mates and with improved condition the fertility increased so the number of foals increased.

The Pony Publicity Group, part of Forest Friendly Farming,(a group set up to promote commoning) has publicised the ponies at many major shows, notably the Horse of the Year Show and the Great Yorkshire. They have held demonstrations at Sparsholt College and Windsor Horse Trials. They have also held a Foal Show before the October Sale and a Youngstock Show before the May Beaulieu Road sale; these were introduced when the saleyard was rebuilt. These shows, where entries have to go through the ring, have been very successful in attracting new buyers if only because they guarantee at least some entries will be halter broken.

Pam Harvey Richards, when President of the New Forest and County Show, inaugurated the President's Challenge, a jumping competition after a first round against the clock in which 16 NF ponies are reduced to 8; in the second round each NF pony is paired with an adult show jumper for a relay against the clock. This is enormous fun and very popular.

8
STUDS

FROM 1912, when Lady Mills was given Bettesthorne Magnet by her husband, till 1952 when she bred her last foal, a colt Bettesthorne Billycock, Lady Mills's Bettesthorne ponies had a remarkable record particularly in the export field. Her outstanding brood mare **Bettesthorne Cautious**, bred 10 foals, 9 of them prizewinners by Jester. Jester, who was bought from the Duchy of Cornwall, was chestnut and the last non Forest whose foals were registered. Cautious was an NPS silver medal winner and descended from the first NF pony exported for breeding to Australia. Cautious's son Bettesthorne Caesar was the sire of the first mare to go to the USA and another of her grandchildren went with her. Her grandson Bettesthorne Hector was the first stallion to go to Sweden and her grandson Beacon Pericles and two of his sisters were among the first to go to Denmark. Another grandson went to Holland. Bettesthorne Caesar and his younger brother Caesar II won many cups at the stallion show and another grandson Bettesthorne Ariel was Mrs Dunlop's foundation stallion so his daughter ended up in New Zealand. Ariel, like my Kate, was Bettesthorne Jessica's foal; Jessica lived to be 34 and her last daughter Bettesthorne Narissa was kept to carry on the line; alas, she won prizes but proved barren. All Lady Mills's ponies were shown by her groom Harry Fudge thus covering a period of 40 years.

The first ponies bred in any number off the Forest were Ted Burry's Mudeford ponies running with **Brookside David** on Stanpit Marsh. When Ted retired, the grazing of Stanpit Marsh was taken over by Don and Joyce Stainer, whose Silverlea pony, **Silverlea Spotlight,** held court there for many years, siring many good ponies, particularly jumpers. Don took over **Mudeford Perdita Grey** with the marsh as it was considered necessary to have one pony that could show newcomers where the fresh water was as most of the pools were salty. Peter Butler has taken over from the Stainers.

Denny Danny, a small pony who started running on the Forest in the '50s and was much loved by his breeder, R. Hoyle, who always referred to him as 'my Danny', was grey and had lovely flat bone and a pretty head. He sired **Merrie Mistral,** foundation sire of the Merrie Stud, and sire of Merrie Mercury. Danny, although short on pedigree, was surely descended from one of the Dyoll Starlight stallions.

Brookside David was probably the most prolific of the stallions on whom the breed was rebuilt after the great reduction caused by the war. David was the only one who did not run the Forest. The demand to be able to breed away from the Forest meant the rule that dams had to have run out for at least a season was dropped; foals reared off the Forest grew bigger. Until 1950 New Forest ponies were classified by the NPS as a 'small breed'. David was about 13.2hh bay, with a wall eye, which he passed to about 1 in 30 of his stock. He had good quarters, legs and bone but was rather short in front. He spent most of his life on Stanpit Marsh, a salt marsh similar to the salt marshes just down the coast to which the ponies had always had access. His son, **Oakley Jonathan**, was the foundation stallion of the Oakley and Beechwood Stud which produced a stream of winners and many of his stock featured in the first wave of exports.

Bettesthorne Cautious, foaled 1924.

Denny Danny.

SILVERLEA SPOTLIGHT
Foaled: 1979
Sire: Silverlea Flash Harry
Dam: Danehurst Gaiety Girl

'Silverlea Stud is now without the wonderful old stallion Silverlea Spotlight who was put down just before Christmas at the age of 24. Though reasonably fit, he was infertile and had spent the summer with one of his beloved ladies, Silverlea Blue Haze II of similar age. She had been with him for eighteen years but this solitary life for them was frustrating. They missed the marsh visitors who had become their friends for such a long time. The two ponies ended their lives together.

'Spotlight was a seventh generation descendant of Brookside David and had been running on Stanpit Marsh, Christchurch from 1984 to 2003, during which time 304 live foals were born.

Don Stainer.

Brookside David.

'A popular nature reserve which attracts thousands of visitors, Stanpit Marsh was also Brookside David's home. Certainly over the twenty years Spotlight was in this beautiful place he gave the visitors immense pleasure. His kindness and generosity will be hard to equal. He was never broken to ride but was quite happy to have excited small children placed on his back to provide "a photo for the family album". On these occasions my late husband and I would walk by, say nothing, but share the same thought "where ignorance is bliss – it's folly to be wise!" Happily over twenty years it never ended in tears. I am sure I would have heard if it had.

'The New Forest Stud Book records show that Spotlight had the highest number of UK registered progeny in recent times, to be precise, 265 with 444 descendants. These numbers could increase considerably when taking into account the 102 of his progeny sold over the years to Canada, Finland, Sweden, Holland, Austria, Spain, Belgium and France. In fact the international database records 680 descendants up to the year 2002. Only two stallions have topped Spotlight's total of 265 in this country – Brookside David, foaled in 1943, and Broomy Slipon, foaled in 1948.

'Spotlight's showing career was limited to two successful outings as a foal, but he was lucky enough to be recognised at the Ponies UK Sire Ratings Awards in 1993. Many of his descendants are extremely talented with out-

standing jumping ability. No doubt he was a people's pony without being pushy – a real gentleman. The visitors on the Marsh will miss his greeting, as I will. It was sad to say goodbye to two such great old servants but a pleasure to have bred and owned them.'
Joyce Stainer

Mrs Rhys's Beechwood ponies and her Commoner groom Charlie Purse's Oakley ponies bred winners, many from the little Forest bred mare **Oakley Bridget**. Her son by Brookside David, **Oakley Jonathan**, after running a few seasons on the Forest, became the stud stallion; his full brother **Oakley Firelight** always ran the Forest. The stud's high spot must have been when **Oakley Stardust** won the in-hand M & M Championship at the Ponies UK summer show, while at the same show her full brother (**Oakley Starlight**) won the M & M Ridden Championship. Stardust was sold to Holland where she was considered too heavy so Mrs Rhys bought her back. Starlight went to Germany where he won a one-day event, being at least 8 in smaller that any other competitor but had the quickest heartbeat recovery after the cross country, where he jumped clear and fast. He was not able to repeat his triumph because they then barred ponies from competing. He also took part in a spectacular demonstration with another NF stallion, **Merrie Musket**, that included airs above the ground. In due

Charlie Purse with Oakley Bridget.

Oakley Starlight wins junior combined training competition in Germany.

course, to Charlie's delight, Starlight too came home and a wonderful season followed when he won nearly everything including qualifying for Olympia. Alas he managed to poleaxe himself on a low branch when turned out that autumn.

OAKLEY BRIDGET

Sire: Forest horse
Dam: Sway Rose
Owner: Mr C. Purse of Beechwood, Burley

'The story of Bridget, a little bay mare standing 12.1 hands, is the story of the family that nearly never was. Bought as a sucker from Mr Blomfield in 1947 for £3 10s. 0d., Bridget ran on the Forest as a yearling. She disappeared for nearly eighteen months and was found in the spring of 1950 in an alley-way at Lymington. Extracted with some difficulty, she was taken home where in May she produced her first foal. She was in such poor condition that she was not put in foal again that year.

'In 1951 Bridget was turned out with Brookside David on the Stanpit Marsh. There she was bullied by all the others, and if transport had been available to remove her she would have come home at once. However, she learned to look after herself and the following April her famous son,

Oakley Jonathan (three times champion stallion) was born. He and his mother were knocked over by a car and required weeks of skilful treatment and stitches before making a complete recovery.'

OAKLEY BRIDGET
NPS 9492
Foaled: 1947
Breeders: W. & G. Blomfield, Pauls Lane, Sway
Owner: Mr C. Purse
1950 Brown Sugar, f, by Forest horse, winner, exported to Holland
1952 Oakley Jonathan III, c, by Brookside David, Champion
1953 Mayfly 6th, f, by Normansland Firefly, winner, exported to Sweden
1954 Gay Henry, c, by David Grey
1955 Sabrina 2nd, f, by David Grey, winner, exported to Holland
  Bred Zuidpools Rufus Von Nomad, by Wigley Nomad, winner, ex
  ported to Sweden
1956 Oakley Ebenezer, c, by Goodenough, winner, exported to Holland
1957 Oakley Davina, f, by Brookside David, winner

Mrs Rhys with Oakley Stardust and Oakley Jenny Wren as foal.

1958 Oakley Colleen, f, by Brookside David, Champion, exported to Holland

1959 Oakley Jenny Wren, f, by Brookside David, Champion

    Bred 1965 Oakley Stardust, f, by Burton Starlight, Champion

    1966 Oakley Starlight, c, by Burton Starlight, winner

    1967 Oakley Starling, c, by Burton Starlight

1960 Oakley Faun, f, by Goodenough, winner

1961 Holyhead,c, by Eastward Bound, GSB winner

1962 Oakley Forebrand, f, by Brookside David, winner exported to France

1963 Oakley Princess May, f, by Deeracres May King

1964 Oakley David, c, by Brookside David

1965 Oakley Firelight, c, by Brookside David

1966 Oakley Pluto,c, by Oakley Poseidon

1967 Oakley Orion, c, by Oakley Poseidon

OAKLEY STARLIGHT

Foaled: 1966

Sire: Burton Starlight

Dam: Oakley Jenny Wren by Oakley Jonathan

Shown as a yearling and won at the Bath & West.

'He ran out with Mr Hayter's mares and was then broken to saddle in 1970. He won three riding classes that year and was ridden champion Mountain & Moorland at the Ponies of Britain. He won both the Stallion in-hand & ridden at the Breed Show and the Dolly Grey Supreme Championship.

'In 1971 he repeated the same success at the ponies of Britain, and was Champion New Forest at the NPS. In 1971 he won the first of his two point-to-point races. He then went to Mrs Illies in Germany where he was most successful in three day events as well as at stud.

'He returned to England in 1980, just in time for the Breed Show where he won the New Forest jumping. He spent that autumn and winter hunting and colt hunting, his two favourite recreations.

'In 1981 he had an astounding season, winning ten cups in-hand and ten in riding classes. He won twelve championships and twenty-three firsts, including three ridden classes and one in-hand class at the Breed Show, and qualifying for the NPS Mountain & Moorland ridden at Olympia.

'The greatest of characters and the most gentle, he enjoyed his last day's colt-hunting the day before the accident that killed him.'

Goodenough started running the Forest and became an enormously

Goodenough.

popular stallion. He was brown and stood no more than 13.0hh; he sired **Priory Starlight,** foundation stallion of Mrs Green's Priory Stud, who in turn sired **Burton Starlight,** foundation sire of Mr Crabb's Burton Stud. Burton Starlight was a great winner himself and eventually was exported to Sweden. Goodenough imparted quality to his stock if not always the best hind leg.

GOODENOUGH

NPS2900
Foaled: 1946
Bred on the forest
Breeder: Mr H.F. Sparks
Owner: Mr F.C. Bennett

'Mr Bennett bought him as a five-year-old and he won the five-year-old cup at the stallion show that year, and went on to stand reserve for the championship to Denny Danny. In 1953, 1954 and 1955 he was champion stallion, winning the Minstead Cup outright. In 1956 he won the Forest class at the ponies of Britain stallion show and went on to take one of the special three premiums for the best of all breeds, one of the very few Forest stallions that have achieved this. Later that year he lost an eye in an accident which put an end to his show career, but in 1957 he gained the Ponies of Britain special award for the Mountain and Moorland stallion whose progeny won the most points at their spring and summer shows.

Setley Poppet.

His progeny have been quite outstanding, nearly all big Forest pony winners seem to be his children, grandchildren or great grandchildren. At the
stallion show in 1968 in a class of 12 top stallions standing at stud, 8 of
the exhibits were direct descendants of Goodenough. Several of his sons
are successful stallions abroad, and one of his daughters, Beacon Celia, was
champion Forest pony at the Royal Show. He was the sire of Priory Starlight, who in turn sired the great champion Burton Starlight whose stock
was so much sought after.'

Goodenough's dam was also very Welsh looking, white, with a long
mane and pretty head, she was known as 'the Ghost' as she flitted
through the trees in Oakley enclosure from which she only emerged
to get in foal. Mrs Jackson always maintained she was out of a mare by
Field Marshall. When so old it was thought she would not make another
winter on the Forest, she was discovered outside the enclosure. Albie
Moore and I set out to try and catch her; she ran from Whitemoor, Turf
Croft, Vereley, Cranesmoor, where she picked her way across the old

firing range where the passage had long since sunk into the bog, we nearly got her in the green lane by Long Pond but she was too quick and shot up the hill by Burbush to Shappen and on to Burley School behind the old Chapel to Woods Corner and back up the side of Oakley, a complete circuit of Burley; we gave up the chase in the bog outside Oakley but caught her next day when she was a very stiff. Waggs Crabb bought her and registered her as Meadend Meadowsweet; it is not certain, but probable, that she was Burton Starlight's grand dam.

SETLEY POPPET
10544 NPS
Foaled: 1953
Sire: Forest horse
Dam: Forest mare
Breeder: H. Sparks, Lower Mead End Farm, Sway
Owner: F.C. Bennett, Ploughlands, Sway

Knightwood Spitfire, in the late 1950s, ridden by Johnny Bradford.

c colt, f filly)
1957 Setley Broome, c, by Goodenough
1959 Setley Pride, c, by Goodenough, exported to Holland
1960 Setley Sundance, c, by Goodenough, winner
1961 Setley Edithmay,f, by Goodenough, champion
> Bred
>> 1965 Setley Denise, f, by Broadley Moonlight, exported to
>> Germany

1966 Setley Fantasy, f, by Goodenough
1962 Setley Sundial, c, by Goodenough, winner
1964 Setley Springtime, c, by Goodenough, winner
1965 Setley Harvest Time, c, by Goodenough, exported to Holland
1966 Setley Poppet II, f, by Goodenough

Knightwood Spitfire, dun 13.2hh, by Brookside Spitfire ex the Weirs' Topsy, was another who started running on the Forest in the '50s before standing at stud. He did particularly well under saddle, ridden by Agister Johnny Bradford. He had bone, more size and good quarters and hind legs. Brookside Spitfire was a grandson of Field Marshall and inherited his chestnut coat and blaze and white stockings; Field Marshall went back to Welton, a TB with 8 Galloway, i.e. pony, crosses. Knightwood Spitfire's dam Topsy was dun by the Highland stallion Clansman 4th, black but from a dun with hazel eyes inherited by Spitfire. Topsy had a white lock at the top of her tail; she was bred by J. Young. The Youngs' Brock ponies are the oldest herd on the Forest. The herd started with nine mares brought as her dowry when Miss Warne, whose family had been commoning on the Forest since the 18th century, married Mr Young. The Youngs never bought a mare until the present generation so all their ponies were descended from the original nine mares.

Bridgelea Candy Cane, foundation stallion of Mrs Stiles Stud in Cambridgeshire, was from the Spitfire line.

The last of the early post-war stallions was **Broomy Slipon**, chestnut when chestnut was a very fashionable colour, and the only one to always run the Forest. For some years a very high proportion of colts coming up for passing were chestnuts, many of these foals by the chunky Broomy Slipon, however a number of these chestnut ponies had round bone and thick under necks. Another bigger chestnut pony, Slipper, with a rubbery neck was certainly a good race pony; a quite disproportionate number of race winners trace to him but not many

Stallion in hand. Newtown Spark and mares at Vereley.

of his fillies gained premiums in the non-hand fed class; however 50% of stallions up for passing in 2001 traced back to him.

Goodenough and **Denny Danny** both ran for some years on the open Forest and both were Society stallions in-hand before standing at stud. Newtown Spark had been stallion in-hand for two seasons and Brookside Spitfire shared a third season with Spark. The Priory and Merrie Studs started within the Forest but later moved away.

The new stud owners had different priorities, for instance Messrs Sibley (Merrie ponies) wanted a pretty head and liked greys so they favoured ponies that went back to the Welsh influence, while Pam Harvey-Richards wanted a pony with bone and better hocks and quarters, she also liked duns, so she went back to those who showed the Highland influence. Since, on the Continent, ponies were only competed by children, and they wanted lighter, leggier animals, there was a loss of type. Stud bred ponies frequently grew a hand bigger than their Forest-bred parents but the biggest often were small horses rather than ponies. Luckily the NPS mixed Mountain and Moorland competitions, particularly the Working Hunter Pony Classes, without an age limit

Beacon Periwinkle by Beacon Pericles ex Beacon Bramble at 1981 breed show.

on the rider, as well as the realization that the ponies are essential for maintaining the traditional character of the Forest – so that the ponies have to be able to thrive on the moors but also be saleable – made the maintenance of type supremely important. Otherwise we wll end up with a homogeneous child's pony but lose the variety, versatility and conservation ability of our heritage ponies.

BEACON PONIES

My first pony was bred by Sir Berkeley Pigott and given to me for my 13th birthday. She was sold because she was a lane creeper. She bred several foals, a lovely filly Bryony, my first show winner, unfortunately killed by a kick from a gelding at three. She also bred the stallion Beacon Briar who ran out on the Forest for many years and Beacon Periwinkle. Bramble was known as the baby Austin - all guts and no brakes. She won the children's race at the point-to-point twice and loved jumping. Every one of her direct descendants who have entered the point-to-point have won or been 2nd and I have the 6th generation descendants today.

BETTESTHORNE KATE
NPS 8794

Foaled: 1947
Sire: Brookside Spitfire
Dam: Bettesthorne Jessica
Breeder: Lady Mills, White House, Biston, Ringwood
Owner: Miss Macnair, Beacon Corner, Burley, winner
1950 Beacon Hotspur, c, by Wildfire 2870 NPS, winner
1952 Beacon Perdita, f, by Denny Danny 2494 NPS, Champion winners
exported to USA
1953 Beacon Touchstone, c, by Newtown Spark 2982 NPS, Champion
winner, exported to Holland
1955 Beacon Miranda, f, by Newtown Spark 2982 NPS , winner, exported
to Denmark
    Bred 2 foals by a Thoroughbred horse and
        1966 Exmoorstaldens Miksey,c, by Yksi, NFS, 10, exported to Sweden
        1967 Exmoorstaldens Winnie the Pooh, f, by Yksi
1957 Beacon Pericles, c, by Denny Danny 2494 NPS Champion winner,
exported to Denmark
1958 Beacon Peto, c, by Eastwood Bound GSB

Bettesthorne Kate.

Beacon Bramble at Breed Show, Burley, 1950s.

1959 Beacon Octavia, f, by Knightwood Spitfire 3121 NPS winner exported to Sweden
 Bred 1964 Beacon Kate, f, by Oakley Jonathan III
1961 Filly by Goodenough (died)
1962 Beacon Celia, f, by Goodenough 2900 NPS Champion winner
 Bred 1966 Beacon Patience, f, by Beacon Briar 3678 NPS

My other foundation mare was Bettesthorne Kate by Brookside
Spitfire ex Bettesthorne Jessica, bred by Lady Mills. She had 16 foals,
all winners, by a number of different stallions. She was ridden but not
much; she could put in a great buck. Many of her foals were exported,
notably Beacon Pericles who became the first stallion in Denmark to
gain the top grade on his and his progenies' merit. Before he left the
Forest he sired Beacon Periwinkle ex B. Bramble.

Beacon Periwinkle was a foal premium winner 3rd as a yearling at the
Breed Show and at 4 she bred a filly and for the next 10 years worked

continually in the riding school and was never lame or sick and never had more than 8 consecutive days off.

The first time she took part in the point-to-point her rider went a very long way round and finished after the following race. She won the next year and was placed in three races that summer when she also won the first of many Jumping Competitions, including 9 consecutive clear rounds with 8 different riders! At one very wet show she came straight from the 13.2hh jump off against the clock to the 11 years and under in another ring, where she came back to a trot after every jump, to allow her first time very nervous rider to get ready for the next jump. Winning the Forest Jumping at the Breed Show was the most satisfactory win but 3rd from a Handy Hunter entry of 105 was perhaps the most difficult; she also won many gymkhana events. She completed several long distance rides and qualified for the Golden Horseshoe doing 42 miles at an average of 8.4 mph but was barred from taking part in the Golden Horseshoe ride itself because she was under 14.0hh.

In 1961 she was a member of the team for the visiting Dutch Children's Jumping Competition as she was in 1971, 1975 and 1981. She won the Open Race at the point-to-point in 1969 and 1971 and was 2nd in 1970 and 1973, she also won the older Children's Race in 1977; on her home ground she took a useful short cut jumping a wide ditch that the only other rider to go with her fell into! She also won trotting and hurdle races and hunter trials culminating in 1975 when she was second in the Performance Competition with 1,200 points having been 5th the year before.

She enjoyed her trips to Olympia, on the first occasion going into the crowded brightly lit arena she made the first circuit crabwise but soon got used to everything – except grunting camels. On the second occasion she carried William Rufus in our pageant and when Rufus was shot by Tyrell and fell among her feet she stood like a rock till taken by Tyrell to make his escape. Unfortunately Tyrell being so relieved to have extracted her without treading on Rufus, forgot Rufus had very short legs and so in mounting went right over her back to land on the other side. She gained bonus points for Hunting, she did 15 seasons with the Buckhounds often carrying 11 stone, colt hunting and 9 years disabled riding - once catching a colt on Whitefield Moor on the way home from RDA. She also represented her breed at the NPS exhibition at the Royal Show where we started by removing 23 Forest flies from under her tail – before she could use them as a secret weapon to disrupt the other breed representatives who would not be used to them!

After 1979 she continued to do her turn in the school, disabled riding and Pony Club, successfully taking part on the Tetrathlon in 1983. She was also the most successful member of the Burley Bunnies Broomstick Polo team. After a gap of 9 years she again won a Hunter Trial Cup for the best NF member in the 11-12 year class in which she was second.

Her 1977 filly Beacon Genista, another marvellous hunting, jumping pony, and point-to-point winner, grew overheight but bred Beacon CandyTuft who qualified for the M & M WHP finals at Malvern also won a point-to-point race and qualified for RC Dressage finals. She also won showing. Her younger full sister, besides also winning the point to point race and the Junior WHP class at the Breed Show, won a championship as a brood mare, bred the stallion B. Mercury, another children's race point-to-point winner and member of the stallions musical ride and the filly Beacon Pieris who loves jumping, a Denbie finalist, WHP qualifier and, like her first cousin, placed point-to-point. She also won the High Jump at Elllingham, clearing 5 ft with a 4ft 9 in spread.

Another line was that of Garth Starflower, a very keen courageous 13 hh pony who won the Open New Forest Race at the point-to-point four times carrying 11st 2 lb although only 13 hh. She loved racing and jumping but whatever you asked she did willingly and never let you down. She would pass anything and was a wonderful harness pony with her daughter being placed 3rd in the inter-breed cones competition (driving) at Windsor (Prince Philip was 4th) this was 20 years after she had been 3rd in hand at the same show. She was often placed in ridden classes. She went to voice which was very useful in harness as she would bring the cart through the gate to order. It was also useful in the riding school and when used for RDA. She adapted perfectly to the rider's capabilities, never trying it on but always gay and willing.

Miss Stephanie Brook was one of the first breeders away from the Forest with her Gosden ponies in the 1950s; the descendants of her good 12.2hh black mare **Poppets** were all called something step(Grey Step, Hop Step, Dance Step, Last Step, etc). She bred ponies for use in her Surrey Riding School where Gail Browrigg, now breeding Leith ponies, was a pupil. Another riding school proprietor, J.Ascolli, bred Foresters to Connemaras because the cross produced hardy, docile animals rather bigger than either of their parents. Another Scottish Equestrian centre is Lomondside, run by the Misses E. and P. Rennie which has been breeding Lomondside ponies for many years including the Olympia qualifier, the stallion **Lomondside Monarch**.

Poppets.

POPPETS
Foundation mare, Miss Brook's stud
8879 NPS
Foaled: 1942
Sire: Forest horse
Dam: Forest mare, champion
Breeder: Unknown
Owner: Miss S.L. Brook, Bramley Riding Stables, Nr Guildford
1948 Metal (crossbred), winner
1951 Top Step, f, by Bettesthorne Hector, winner
        Bred
        1956   Highenough, f, by Goodenough, winner
1953 Grey Step, c, by David Grey, winner
1954 Hop Step, f, by Bettesthorne Hector, winner
        Bred
        1958   Gosden Thomas, c, by Denny Danny, winner
        1960   Cricket, c, by Bubbly (crossbred), winner
        1961   Gosden Nicholette, f, by Hotspur Nicholas Nixon,

Ridden Champion and Olympia Qualifier, Mr & Mrs Large's Peveril Peter Piper, with his breeder, Mrs Betty Haycock and rider Caroline Large.

    champion
    1962 Chanticleer, c, by Chantain (crossbred), winner
    1964 Gosden Pickle, f, by Hotspur Nicholas Nixon, win
    ner
    1966 Gosden Pirouette, c, by Setley Sundance
    1967 Gosden Jon's Step, c, by Oakley Jonathan III, win
    ner
1955 Black Step, c, by Bettesthorne Hector, winner
1956 (Filly died due to accident)
1957 Dance Step, f, by Denny Danny, winner
    Bred
    1961 Tantany Petronella, f, by Oakley Jonathan III
    1964 Tantany Step Stately, f, by , exported to Sweden
1958 Penny Step, f, by Denny Danny, winner, exported to Sweden
    Bred
    1963 Priory Fairy Tale, f, by Priory Starlight VII
    1964 Priory Brown Pansy, f, by Priory Paint Box

1960 May Step, f, by Deeracres Mayking, champion
     Bred
        1966   Gosden Pepper, f, by Knightwood Spitfire, winner
1961 Small Lord, c (crossbred)
1962 Niggerstep of Bridgelea, c, by Merrie Minstrel, champion
1964 Last Step, c, by Hotspur Nicholas Nixon, winner

Barbara Stiles, a well known Mountain and Moorland judge and Cambridgeshire farmer's wife, brought her three daughters for holidays in the Forest and, as well as buying ponies for the girls to ride, went to the sales and bought some good old mares whose owners felt that they were getting rather old to winter on the Forest. On the farm they bred several more foals. To start with she borrowed the stallion Beacon Briar, who had run the Forest many years but always came home at the start of the hunting season; he blotted his copybook by not recognizing dykes as boundaries; he went swimming, surfacing with someone else's mares! Barbara then bought **Bridgelea Candy Cane** who proved an outstanding stallion. The outstanding pony from this Fijal stud must be **Fijal Prelude**, three times supreme Champion at the Breed Show.

A number of Commoners breed some ponies on the Forest and some on the holding: Owen Dibden's Ashley ponies and recently the Pidgley's Sheepwash ponies are examples. Susan Shaw, the Sibley's daughter, has acquired a piece of land with Forest rights so that she can again run two mares on the Forest.

At the start of the twenty-first century Mrs Haycock's Peveril stud, which began about 1950, heads the list. Founded on another small mare, Peveril Petrina, bought as a child's pony for her son, she bred **Peveril Pipette**, who won, among much else, the open 13.2hh brood mare class at the Royal Show. This stud has bred a long line of winners including the stallions Peveril Pickwick, Peveril Peterborough, Peveril Probus and the top elite stallion Peveril Peter Piper, foundation stallion of the Willoway Stud where he sired many show winners and some outstanding jumping ponies. In 2005 this stud is still breeding winners.

The Willoway stud's foundation stallion **Peveril Peter Piper,** another small pony with a lovely head and sire of show ponies and jumpers, has been the outstanding leader in the Elite scheme. Another stallion with the Peveril Prefix and an outstanding show record who can also jump is **Peveril Peterborough.**

PEVERIL PETRINA FOUNDATION MARE, PEVERIL STUD

9580 NPS

Foaled: 1949

Breeder: W. House, Ravensbeck Farm, East End, Lymington

Owner: Mr & Mrs P.B. Haycock, Newtown Peveril House, Sturminster Marshall, Wimborne

1954 Easter Frolic PBA(part bred Arab) winner

1958 Peveril Pippette, f, by Priory Starlight, champion

> Bred
>
> 1961 Peveril Hamilton Plum, f, by Beacon Pericles, winner, exported to Holland
>
> 1962   Peveril Paree, f, by Priory Gay Gordon, champion
>
> 1964   Peveril Probus, c, by Oakley Jonathan III, exported   to Denmark
>
> 1965   Peveril Pickwick, c, by Oakley Jonathan III, champion
>
> 1966   Peveril Personality, f, by Niggerstep of Bridgelea, winner
>
> 1967   Peveril Percival, c, by Niggerstep of Bridgelea,   winner

1962 Peveril Peter Pan, c, by Priory Starlight VII, winner

1963 Peveril Pollyanna, f, by Deeracres May King, exported to Holland

1965 Peveril Parana, f, by Oakley Jonathan III

1966 Peveril Peeress, f, by Canford Count, winner

1967 Peveril Pinmoney, f, by Luckington Lancer

PEVERIL PETERBOROUGH (2005)

Sire: Deeracres Franco

Dam: Peveril Taylor Maid

Breeder: Mrs E. Haycock

Owner: Sabine Andree-Parsons

'Peveril Peterborough is probably the most successful Performance New Forest pony to date, having won over 200 championships in ridden, in-hand, WHP classes and also excelling in dressage and show jumping. He has always applied himself to whatever task was in hand with good grace and enthusiasm (sometimes a bit too much), and even after having been shown extensively for 15 years has remained sound and keen.

'It was a great honour for him when Princess Anne presented him with the Elite Performance Pony Rosette at the New Forest County Show where he also won the Ridden NF Stallion class for the eleventh time (out of 12 attempts). He also won the *Horse and Hound* cup for the Ridden

Champion for a record 9 times, and was one of the winning pair in the Presidents' Challenge again. At the Breed Show, Peterborough, he has won the Stud Stallion In-Hand Championship 5 times, Ridden Stallion 9 times and been Supreme Champion 4 times. He has qualified for Olympia 8 times (where he is still the highest placed New Forest with 3rd) and for Wembley final 7 times.

'In 1993 he achieved what no pony has achieved before or since, namely to qualify for the "big three" in the same year - the Creber in-hand at Wembley, Olympia and the NPS WHP final at Wembley. Peveril Peterborough has certainly been a horse in a million to me, and his regular rider, Fiona Biddle, with whom he struck up a terrific partnership spanning 10 years.

'Hopefully his progeny will continue to do well and may he produce many more in his retirement. His favourite music seems to be Tina Turner - being a bit of a party animal, and one of her songs sums him up - "simply the Best"! In my eyes anyway.'

His son Sabina's Gold Sovereign Grade 3 jumping stallion and Olympia and HOYS WHP qualifier is his best son who is now also siring winners.

Up till 1949 New Forest ponies were classified by the NPS as a small breed along with the Exmoors and Dartmoors and even today ponies bred and reared on the Forest average just over 13.0hh.

Studs by selective breeding and increased nutrition have improved the general appearance of the ponies and considerably increased their size, though occasionally with a loss of elasticity of movement. Better training has shown the ponies' enormous potential. However there is a fine balance: dangerous roads and a general lack of time means ponies are boxed to rallies, meets and competitions where in times past they would have been hacked. Many are kept in small electric fenced paddocks, with higher nutrition and, as with the children, this leads to much too fat ponies with laminitis and puffy joints.

Ponies have a low boredom level, they need stimulation and enough to do. Bad behaviour is often due to not enough work. I once had two young ponies in the Vicarage field. The field was rather small and surrounded by garden where nothing much was going on. The vicar had planted a row of runner beans supported on poles tied together with green twine, at right angles to the fence and right up to it. One of the ponies discovered that by pulling the end of the green twine the furthest post pulled out of the ground and fell against the next in line. Another pull and the next pole fell; soon the whole row was flattened. Unlike horses, ponies like variety; in the wild they have to

Peveril Petrina.

eat a variety of plants at different times of year. Forest-bred ponies are lucky, they have variety, the space and company to be able to really gallop up and down hill and over different surfaces which strengthens bones and joints.

All breeds are tending to lose their smaller ponies although these often have more quality and type; the temperament of most NF ponies makes them ideal for beginners. The taller, finer ponies would be unlikely to winter on the moors and the importance of the ponies for conservation grazing is essential for the survival of the traditional character of the Forest. All this shows the vital importance of maintaining true type and this cannot be stressed enough.

Barbara Stiles bought one of Fiona Stephens's filly foals from Fiona's outstanding brood mare Amberslade Brownie and from her bred the three times supreme champion **Fijal Prelude**, Mrs Hadwin's foundation stallion Fijal Maestro and Fiona Biddle's Fijal Encore; Fiona now carries on the line.

From about 1960 for some 30 years Mrs Betty Gwinner's **Luckington** ponies featured at most shows. Her as usual very small foundation mare **Luckington Double Chance** bred nine foals that all won or were exported or both. Her daughter Luckington Double Diamond carried on the good work.

LUCKINGTON DOUBLE CHANCE
400NFM
Sire: Forest horse
Dam: Forest mare
Foaled: 1955
Breeder: G. Kitcher, Chapel Lane, East End, Lymington

Fijal Prelude.

Owner: Mrs Gwinner, Woodcutters, Bashley, New Milton
1957 Lilly of Monkshorn, f, by Monkshorn Bumbo, exported to Holland
     Bred 1962   Fantail of Luckington, f, by Rufus II who bred:
              1966 Luckington Locket, f, by Goodenough
              1967 Luckington Pintail, f, by Goodenough
1960 Luckington Leap Year, f, by Forest horse, winner, exported to Holland
1961 Luckington High Star, f, by Oakley Jonathan III, Champion, exported
to Sweden
     Bred 1967 colt
1962 Luckington Good Gracious, f, by Goodenough, winner, exported to
Denmark
     Bred 1965 f, Luckington Goodtime by Deeracres Summertime,
exported to Holland
          1966 c, Luckington Minstrel, by Niggerstep of Bridgelea, winner
          1967 f, by Oakley Jonathan III
1963 Luckington Lancer ,c, by Goodenought, Champion
1964 Luckington Splash, f, by Goodenough, Champion
1965 Luckington Leader, c, by Oakley Jonathan III, winner, exported to
France
1966 Luckington Lucy, f, by Burton Starlight, winner

Luckington Double Chance.

Willoway Pipers Gold enjoys a swim.

1967 Luckington Double Diamond, f, by Goodenough, winner

Present successful studs include Mr and Mrs Large's Willoway ponies whose Peveril Peter Piper has bred numerous champions including the stallions Willoway Pipers Gold and Willoway Double Gold and 2005 Breed Show Olympia qualifier Willoway Pipers Paragon.

Waggs Crabb was an Avon valley farmer unusually breeding New Forest ponies; in the years after World War II he bred **Burton Starlight** who carried all before him both in-hand and ridden and was the sire of Oakley Stardust and Oakley Starlight. Burton Starlight was by Priory Starlight who was by Goodenough; eventually Starlight was exported to Sweden and June Whitham acquired Waggs's best brood mare, **Burton Honey**. From Honey June has produced a dynasty of excellent ponies still a force to be recognised in the showring today.

The Farriers stud is owned by Mr and Mrs Simon Young, who have bred **Farriers Drummer Boy**, another Olympia qualifier who won the small open ridden class at the breed show no less than ten times and many championships. Their present stallion **Farriers Fingerprint**,

Sabina's Gold Sovereign owned by Mrs S. Andree Parsons ridden by Gina Williams.

another son of Peveril Peter Piper, has a wonderful temperament and not only wins under saddle but also dressage classes as well as enjoying colt-hunting and barrel racing. They also run ponies on the Forest including their share of the Brock ponies. Simon's brother James and his wife Trudy bred Brock Bewitched, the first Forest bred supreme champion at the breed show for 20 years, and what is more she has done it twice and James gave her away as a birthday present! The ponies they breed from bought-in ponies carry the prefix **Tremley**.

Gill Wright's **Burley** ponies have done very well; she bred the stallion Burley Branston, who runs with John and Wendy Adams's mares, temporarily got in off the Forest to run with him. Gill has the attractive small stallion Burley Showman, who will hopefully revive the fortunes of the little New Forest ponies, and Burley Gold Blend, now owned by Nikki Kemp.

Peveril Peterborough, having had an outstanding performance career ridden by Fiona Biddle, now stands at her stud, whilst his most successful son, Sabine's Gold Sovereign, another Olympia and Horse of the Year Show Mountain and Moorland qualifier, stands with his breeder, Sabine Andree Parsons.

Nick Williams has the Horse of the Year Show Mountain and Moorland Working Hunter Pony qualifier and very neat jumper Peronne Palaver, standing on the Isle of Wight.

The Booth family from Cornwall stand another stallion who wins Working Hunter Pony classes, Woodrow Portman, bred by June Whitham, twice winner of the Performance Competition.

Mary Bryant's Wayland Cranberry has several times qualified for Olympia and is an outstanding dressage pony, finishing 9th overall in the riding clubs dressage to music championships where most of those placed were horses; Cranberry's son Wayland Loganberry, also in 2005, qualified as a sports pony stallion.

Woodrow Honey's Delightful.

Mrs Hadwin's **Highfox** ponies fly the flag in the north where Rae Turner also breeds a pony or two.

Commoners who also breed on their holdings besides the formentioned Pidgleys and Owen Dibdin, include the Humble's **Lovely Hill** ponies. Commoners who breed almost all on the Forest include R.& J. Stride's **Rushmoor** ponies; they bred the very successful Horse of the Year Show Working Hunter Pony Rushmoor Sunset. Their stallion Knightsway Billy Boy was five times winner of the champion Forest running stallion. One of their principal rivals is the van Hennicks, whose East End Breezer, before going to Holland, gained the highest mark of any for his walk at the stallion performance testing. They also bred Buckland Dragonslayer, sire of Brock Bewitched. Mrs van Hennick is the daughter of Mr House, who bred Monkshorn Trooper, the only Forest running stallion to feature in the first list of Elite stallions. B. Wilson bred the outstanding little mare Bakeburn Cindy.

Demonstration at Sparsholt, 2004: three generations of Young family on Farriers Fingerprint, Farriers Drummer Boy and Bell, showing variation of size in the breed.

Brock Bewitched

Major Forest breeders include R. H. Bennett (Mockbeggar ponies) and D. Dibdin (Millersford ponies).

9
PONIES & PEOPLE

LORD ARTHUR CECIL WAS CHAIRMAN of the Polo Society, predecessor of the NPS, in the early 20th century. He lived at Lymington and, along with Rev. Dale, was the pony authority of the day. He was one of the founders of the Society for the Improvement of New Forest Ponies 1891. He believed all British native ponies had a common ancestry but were in-bred on their native habitats and the way to improve them was to take stallions from one area to another. Hence the mixture of breeds in the early stud books. In fact he was wrong on both counts.

Lord Lucas, who lived at Picket Post, was the first Chairman of the Burley & District New Forest Pony & Cattle Society; he had lost a leg in South Africa but this did not stop him show jumping or riding his 13.2hh NF pony 'The Nun', who carried his 12stone 7lb into 3rd place in the 1912 point-to-point. They also won several matches and the pony was also 3rd at the breed show 1909 as a three-year-old. Lord Lucas travelled the country looking for stallions on Exmoor, Dartmoor and Wales, where he bought three by Dyoll Starlight. Some, like Picket Hermit, were part TB as he considered TB to be the cream of the equine species and the more cream the better the milk! He used the prefix Picket on all his bought-in ponies as well as those he bred, other people often used the pony's haunt as a prefix.

In the first Annual Report he wrote:

> We have a breed unsurpassed in hardiness and endurance. To know that, look at the ponies of the New Forest Scouts at the end of a 50 mile day in camp. Some horses were lying down dead beat and refusing their feed, the Foresters, some only three-year-

Arthur Cecil.

Lord Lucas.

olds stood up and emptied their nosebags, not one being sick or sorry. A wild four-year-old running the Forest will teach you the same thing after you have tried to catch him and he has galloped your corn fed hunter to a standstill. The breed produces admirable trappers with good paces and beautiful natural action, first rate draught and sometimes the very perfection of boy's Hunters. The son of a member of our committee is to be seen holding his own with a Leicestershire field on a 13hh Forester bred on the Forest and reared on the richer pasture of the Avon Valley. Not all can perform such feats, were it so there would be no need for our Society. In spite of the NF pony Asc., which looks after the sires and individual breeders like Lord Arthur Cecil, too few ponies show the best qualities of their breed. We felt the best chance of success lay in trying to get the whole body of commoners to unite and take common action for the improvement of the breed. It is our dream that one day we shall count every commoner among our members!

Besides setting ourselves to breed the stamp of pony the purchasing public wants we have to let them know we have such ponies. It was only when the Welsh formed their Asc. and Stud Book that Welsh ponies became so widely recognized and sought after. We have started a Stud Book, which will prove the best means of advertising that we have a recognized breed. It will do more when it records that the dam and great dam have been prizewinners, it will stamp them as a strain worth perpetuating. We know there are many such strains, we also know of famous old strains that have been scattered, sold and lost sight of. We have introduced a system of premiums to help commoners resist the temptation to sell the best.

Lord Lucas was killed in the Great War. Maurice Baring wrote of him:

> Oh Liberal heart fast rooted in the soil,
> Oh lover of ancient freedom and proud toil,
> Friend of the gypsies and all wandering song.
> The Forest's nursling and the favoured child of woodland wild –
> It is well with you,
> Among the chosen few,
> Among the very brave, the very true.

Rev. T. Dale, 1848-1923, was President of the Society for the Improvement of NF ponies (the Lyndhurst Society) 1911-12. He was a keen hunting man; there were few packs of fox or stag hounds with which he was not closely acquainted. He had great knowledge and appreciation of horse and hound and their pedigrees, was a pioneer of the Polo Society and had made a close study of the native breeds. Here in the Forest he became patriarch and oracle to both societies. He judged the stallions for many years and never forgot a pony he had judged. He felt that when ponies were making little money Commoners just left them on the Forest to get on with it and this was beneficial as it encouraged the survival of the fittest.

Sir Berkeley Pigott was appointed Hon. Sec. to the Burley Society in 1935 and the new joint Society in 1938. Ponies' prefix Shobley. He held everything together through World War II, also being Hon. Sec. to the Commoners' Defence, Rhinefield Polo Club, NF Pony Club, etc. Each Society had a different room in his house and he migrated between them. He revived the NPS from a very bad patch after the war. He played polo on his home-bred Forest pony Shobley Hazel by Minstead Hazel ex-Lady Roe, a little brown 13.1hh mare. Minstead Hazel had been

Sir Berkeley Pigott

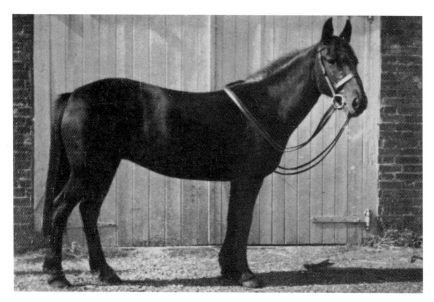

Shobley Hazel.

stallion in-hand in 1938. Hazel was no show pony; she was known as 'rabbit ears', but though enormous they were always pricked. She had a filly foal in 1944 and was then broken in by Ron Ings. With little schooling she took to polo straight away and in 1947 and '48 went with the Rhinefield team to Roehampton holding her own with the bigger ponies, riding anyone off. She got a good write up in *The Times*. She has given many a beginner their first taste of polo and seems to have enjoyed every minute although colt hunting was her favourite sport. She never seemed to tire carrying 12 stone over 25 miles and more. In the trailer she preferred to travel backwards with her head over the tail board; she had to wear hobbles as her one idea was to get everywhere as quickly as possible and the trailer got hammered in her efforts to speed it up. She was never sick or sorry and very tolerant of people and other ponies.

Sir Berkeley was Hon. Sec. till 1957, when he handed over to Mrs Parsons and became Chairman instead; having lost an eye to shingles, he took to wearing an eye patch. He was an excellent Chairman and for some years a Verderer.

Miss Jackson was elected to the Burley Society Council in 1924, and was the only woman on it! She and her sister started breeding NF

Olga Golby on Brookside Judy, 1936.

ponies soon after World War I; Olga Golby, the daughter of the family groom, was adopted by the sisters and with them taught children to ride. Sadly the older sister was kicked on the head and died. Olga agreed to stay as long as the remaining sister kept the ponies. They shared the prefix Brookside and bred many good ponies including the stallions **Brookside David**, sold to Ted Burry, and **Brookside Spitfire**. Brookside Judy and Brookside Tommy Tucker won many ridden classes in the 1930s. Brookside Marcia, whom they drove through the war, was

Beacon Moonrise, Brookside Judy's 11.3hh granddaughter.

Marcia III doing war work.

the dam of Brookside Olivia, who, although only 12.2hh, won many ridden classes after the war for her adult owner Hilary Kircus. Young Judy, sold to Mr Tennant, was a big winner as was Tessa, a beautiful liver chestnut if a trifle temperamental. Olga always referred to Miss Jackson as her 'old dear': she came to shows in a silk dress and green boots with wooden soles and orange laces. She was not a good loser and could be very grumpy if she had not done well.

Judy's last foal Brookside Juliette, only 12.2hh and black, was known as Imp because she was usually the other side of the fence from her dam. She had the deepest whicker I have ever heard; we called it Imp's hooter. She became an excellent child's hunter and bred Beacon Julian, a premium stallion for many years, who was also regularly hunted by his adult owner Mrs Mackworth Praed although they only had two good eyes between them. Juliette also foaled Beacon Moonrise, also black but only 11.3hh, a great character and a wonderfully versatile first pony. Moonrise was bred on the Forest, she was brought home, a distance of some 5 miles, tied round her grand dam's neck. That halter broke her and thereafter she would tie up anywhere. Juliette had 14 foals, several exported; she spent her later life entirely on the Forest and no one ever saw her ribs. Unlike Juliette, her half brother Brookside Punch, also black, grew overheight but was a great success as a boys do-everything pony with the Ellis family.

One of Miss Jackson's rivals was Anne Mcgrath who started showing her pony Minstead Gay Girl, bought from the Browns, before the war, and is still showing her descendants in 2005. She bred the champion stallion Vernons Vespers and many other winners. Vespers was one of only two New Forest to qualify for Lloyds Bank champion of all breeds, the other being Deeracres Picasso, owned by James Young and Trudy Nineham and bred by Mrs Parsons.

Frank Shutler started as groom about 1910 to Lord Lucas; he bred many ponies on the Forest including **Priory Pippin,** foundation mare of Christine Green's Priory Stud. Pippin was under 12.2hh, chestnut and a lovely mover; having been successfully shown herself she went on to breed Priory Pink Petticoats, the first winner of the Performance competition and many more Championships, and several more winning foals. Frank became an Agister and a Pony Society Council member; he was vice-chairman for many years. He was also a popular judge; as he had very good hands, every pony went well when he rode it. His daughter **Joan Wright** also became a much respected judge. In 1947 her lovely pony **Slowlass II** was chosen to represent the produce of

Frank Shutler on Carmelite.

Vernons Vesper, Kent County Show 1982.

a New Forest mare and a TB sire at the National Horse Association's lecture given by Col. Faudle-Phillips at Knightsbridge Barracks. The other representatives were Dolly XXX, a little 12.2hh child's pony, Molly XVII, both bred by Bertie Peckham, another very small mare, who won the Commoners and Small Brood Mare at the breed show year after year, and Brookside Firelight, a 14.2hh gelding known as Goliath, a very deep pony with bone and substance, an excellent hunter and twice winner of the Cob Class at Salisbury whilst his daughter Dolly Grey was winning the Forest class. The polo pony Shobley Hazel and a nondescript pony completed the team. Mrs Parsons and Sir Berkeley also spoke to an audience of 200 people.

PRIORY PIPPIN Foundation mare, Priory stud

8351 NPS
Foaled: 1944
Sire: Forest horse
Dam: Burley Bracken
Breeder: the late F. Shutler
Owner: Mrs C.M. Green, Meadowside, Littlefield Green, White Waltham, Berks
1951 Priory Bandbox, f, by Brookside David, champion
   Bred
     1957 Priory Watersprite, f, by Priory Starlight VII
     1958 Priory Piper, c, by Denny Danny
     1959 Priory Minstrel, c, by Goodenough
     1960 Priory Playbox, c, by Priory Starlight VII
     1961 Priory Pollyflinders, f, by Priory Starlight VII
     1961 Priory Parasol, f, by Priory Gay Gordon
       Bred 1966 Priory Peach Blossom by Burton Sunlight
           1967 Priory Sunshade by Burton Sunlight
     1963 Priory Pantomime, c, by Setley Sundance
     1964 Priory Sunhat, c, by Priory Top Hat
     1965 Stafford Hat Band, c, by Priory Top Hat, winner, exported to Denmark
     1966 Stafford Bandolier, c, by Priory Blue Peter of Rockford, winner
1954 Musical Box, c, by David Grey, winner
1955 Sweet Sue II, f, by Brookside David, winner, exported to Sweden
1956 Firefly VII, c, by Brookside David

Priory Pippin.

1957 Cross-bred foal
1958 Priory Pandora, f, by Priory Starlight VII, winner, exported to Sweden
    Bred
    1962   Priory Pavlova, f, by Priory Gay Gordon, exported
    to Sweden
    1963   Priory Pageant, c, by Setley Sundance
    1964   Priory Polonaise, f, by Hillfield Blue Peter, winner
    1955   Priory Prunella, f, by Hillfield Blue Peter, winner,
    exported to Sweden
1959 Priory Pirouette, f, by Goodenough, winner
1960 Priory Paintbox, c, by Priory Starlight VII, exported to Germany
1961 Priory Mr Pastry, c, by Knightwood Palamino, winner, exported to
Holland
1962 Priory Pink Petticoats, f, by Priory Gay Gordon, supreme champion
1967
1963 Priory Warpaint, c, by Burton Starlight
1964 Priory Pirouette II, f, by Hillfield Blue Peter, winner
1965 Priory Pepperpot, c, by Hillfield Blue Peter
1966 Priory Peter Pan, c, by Hillfield Blue Peter
1967 Priory Patch Box, c, by Burton Starlight

Joan was a popular Society Chairman for many years, for some time also doing the job of Hon. Treasurer. She was very diplomatic and a

Theresa Wright on Sovereign.

brilliant show commentator, who made a point of finding out about all the entries beforehand. Her three daughters inherited her interest in the ponies. As children they were well known in the ring with their consistent jumping pony **Sovereign**, bred on Burley Lawn by Forest Horse out of Ben Watts's good mare Queenie 15th, whose dam Missie was regularly placed in the Forest Fed Class. Sovereign had a generous head and not the best back end, but a zest for living. He was a lively ride and not always easy to catch but the smallest child could be entrusted to his care in the box. A five-year-old was once found in his box with a foot on each hock vainly trying to mount by climbing his tail! Both were quite happy. He first showed his potential by jumping out of Lymington pound. The Wright family acquired him as a five-year-old and the following year he won the Forest jumping at the Breed Show. He subsequently won it twice more; he was 2nd in the Child's Hunter, attended Pony Club camp and appeared in fancy dress at the Ringwood Carnival. He finished the year by winning the Children's Race at the Boxing Day point-to-point by 20 lengths and then completed a lap of honour round Whitefield Moor. He represented his branch at the Pony Club one day event finals, where he was the smallest competitor but was clear in the cross country and show jumping, ending up 7th overall. He nearly killed himself eating baby turkey food on his annual escape but was 2nd in a 14.2hh jumping class only three days later. The following year one of Joan's daughters, Gill, then aged ten, took over from her older sister Theresa. He won £350 jumping, a huge sum in the 1960s, and sometimes jumped 12 clear rounds in a day. Gill took over from her mother as Chairman of the Society, she also became Chairman of the NPS Mountain and Moorland Committee and also, like her mother, is a very well known Forest and M & M judge whilst her sister Theresa is the Society's computer wizard, organizing the web site and the Stud Book.

David Stagg, a Verderer, had undertaken the huge job of putting the whole Stud Book back to 1890s on computer during which he found 23 sets of twins, five of which were correct, one remarkable mare having five live foals in three years. He had also instituted the controversial filly premium scheme. He wanted to use the scheme to gain information on bloodlines, fertility and hardiness from the computer records. He therefore raised the age every year till all mares were included and the standard being only acceptable condition did nothing to improve quality but the information just beginning to come through was interesting. Unfortunately at this point the Verderers allowed unregistered mares to take part and this finally killed the scheme, because the cash was spread so thin it no longer covered the cost of the marking fee and owners lost interest. At least ten years and a lot of interpretation would have been necessary, for instance he found the over 20 age group had 100% fertility! This was due, not to mares becoming more fertile with age, but to the fact that there were not many of them, and obviously only those who were hardy regular breeders were kept that long.

Mrs Parsons (Deeracres prefix) succeeded Sir Berkeley as Hon. Sec. of the Pony Society for nine years(1951-1960). During her term of office the NPS got very slow at processing registrations and printing the Stud Book so in 1960 the Society decided to publish its own, which has come out annually ever since. Vols 9 and 11 had interesting re-entries of mares with their progeny: Priory Pippin had 15 foals recorded whilst Oakley Bridget had 17. Mrs Parsons ran the stallion Deeracres Winston Churchill on the Forest and ran mares out before the war. Whilst in office she bred the stallions Deeracres Mayking and Deeracres Summertime, both later exported, Deeracres Franco, and Deeracres Picasso, who qualified for the Lloyds Bank all breeds Championship at the Horse of the Year Show. She showed Deeracres Sally and Garth Remus as a pair; among many other successes, they won the Fancy Dress at Ponies of

Deeraces Sally and Garth Remus, at the Royal International Horse Show, 1960 (spot the ghost!).

Britain Show. This pair was lent to the Queen to teach Prince Andrew to drive. Her best known champion was probably the mare **Deeracres Mayqueen** but Betty Parsons found she was minding too much if she was beaten and thought this showed a wrong sense of values so she gave up showing.

Eleanor Dunlop was a great friend of Betty Parsons, a Pony Society council member and panel judge, and breeder of ponies with the Bullhill prefix; she bought the stallion Bettesthorne Ariel, bred by Lady Mills. Eleanor eventually went to live in New Zealand taking a stallion and five mares with her from where she sold a colt to Australia.

Lady Mills bred NF ponies for most of the 20th century. Her first pony, Bettesthorne Magnet, 13.1hh, foaled 1908, being her foundation mare. Lady Mills's husband brought in the chestnut Dartmoor stallion Jester in 1930, one of the last outsiders admitted to the Stud Book and sire of Bettesthorne Caesar. After the war she bred Bettesthorne Hector, one of the first ponies to go to Sweden and my foundation mare Bettesthorne Kate, 13.0hh, dam of 16 foals, all winners.

Another pre-war breeder was **Miss Blackmoor**, who bred Griselda and sold her daughter Dolores to **Ted Burry**; he showed in the 1930s, and with the produce of Brookside David was by far the most successful breeder in the immediate post-war era. Unfortunately he registered the mares he put to David without pedigree to start with. He had a very old trailer much given to punctures, the tyres it used being no longer made. In this he took his ponies to shows all over the south. His favourite show was the Royal; at that time the classes were for mares and fillies but they offered a male championship for which the only pony eligible was the highest placed yearling colt who might have been beaten by 5 fillies. No yeld mares (mares not in foal), no geldings and no stallions were shown. Ted won this championship several times and would display the rosette and championship card prominently when the foreign buyers came; it helped him sell several yearling colts rather well. His daughter Olive had the best ponies but as she suffered from car sickness she never ventured far afield.

Ron Ings was born and lived all his life in the Forest he loved. He had his first pony when he was eight and rode it bareback. Rejected for military service in 1939, he joined the Home Guard and worked for the Forestry Commission hauling timber with a team of horses. Since we were assured enough timber had been extracted from the Forest to

Eleanor Dunlop at the Burley Show in the late '50s.

Ron Ings with Gosden Top Step and Wainsford West Wind.

construct a bridge from London to New York nine feet wide and two inches thick, this was some haul!

Ron was an Agister and senior Agister for ten years but his real talent was for training horses and ponies. He collected everyone's problems and his quiet, calm but firm handling usually won through. He managed to break Brookside Spitfire, who had spent the first 23 months of his life mainly in Ossemsley, at that time virtually unfenced. He had hardly seen a human and was very wild and highly strung, so when he came to be caught to be passed as a stallion he led everyone a great chase. When finally shut in a loose box he attempted to jump out through the barred window! Attempts to lead and lunge him usually resulted in his setting his strong neck and charging straight ahead; even in a very confined space he got away till Ron arrived with his large solid cob. Spitfire was tied round the cob's neck and taken for a two-hour haul at the end of which Ron backed him with no problems. Soon he was using him to round up Delgety's cattle and could leave him tied to a tree; he always taught ponies to tie up, calling those who pulled back 'ladies ponies'. As Spitfire panicked if his rider was at all nervous, very few other people could ride him. A year after he was returned to his owner, they had problems with a colt at the Stallion Show and asked Ron to take Spitfire; on seeing Ron Spitfire whickered and was obviously delighted to be reunited with an old fiend.

My chief recollection of Ron is seeing him, on a fine summer Saturday, driving up the A3 with his cob between the shafts, one pony tied alongside and two more tied on behind and a string of cars stretching out into the distance behind them. Alas! We shall not see his like again.

'**Don Stephens** (prefix **Furzey Lodge**) is a remarkable person and a true gentleman, respected by all the Forest Community, who remains fiercely independent at 83 years young. He still keeps ponies and cattle with the help of his extended family, who have inherited his love of the Forest way of life. Don's involvement with ponies is due to his friend Bob Kitcher and with his encouragement he bought his first pony, a yearling filly that came from Bob's father.

'Don next bought two mares for £6 and £7 with 'sucker yearling' colts on them. They were sold at Beaulieu Road Sale, one made a guinea and a quarter, the other a guinea and a half. About that time Don bought a big colt for 37/6d, called Nobber, who was out of a semi-carthorse by a Forest stallion. Nobber was gelded and broken in at 3 years old, and he was a real character. Anyone could ride him, Mrs Parsons used him to pull her gypsy caravan and he also pulled the grass cutter. Hubert Forward was the Agister in those days and Don used to go round with him, to find the ponies that had been impounded for straying into Lymington. They used to take the ponies to Sam Drodge's holding at Pilley. After putting halters on the ponies, they would tie them together and finally attach them to Nobber and let them loose. Nobber would bring them back home via the Forest to Furzey! Sometimes they needed the gorse prickles removed from their legs when they got there. The first registered New Forest Pony Don owned was called Crockford Pride. The total number of mares he owned slowly increased including some bought from Fred Kitcher at East End.

'Don's involvement with the registered ponies increased over the years, and he was elected a member of Council in 1949. He became a respected Breed Society Judge and also was on the Standards Committee for the New Forest Verderers. Don's comment on today's judging is, "They don't pay enough attention to the hind quarters when assessing a pony." He was a regular course-setter for the Boxing Day point-to-point but never raced in it. The Furzey Lodge ponies

'Bunny McGrath' presenting the Forest bred Champion Trophy to Furzey Lodge Anthea with owner and breeder Don Stephens.

exerted a strong influence on the open Forest and Don and his wife Fiona became a power to be reckoned with in the Show Ring, winning many championships. Don's all-time favourite pony is Brownie of Amberslade. Her most famous daughter was Woodfidley Soft Music, who was sold to Mrs Barbara Stiles, after much persuasion! Soft Music and Bridgelea Candy Cane produced some outstanding Fijal ponies, including the champion mare Fijal Prelude. "Brownie of Amberslade was the best mare ever, she won the brood mare class five times at Romsey Show," Don recalls. Another pony that did well was his chestnut stallion Lyndhurst Springtime.

'Don still runs good stallions on the Forest: Furzey Lodge Benjamin, Bruno, Zennica and Neil, the latter kept in to use at home for the last few years. Don is particularly pleased with his pretty grey stallion Zennica, who is never out of the ribbons when shown. In January 2005, a total of 476 Furzey Lodge ponies have been registered with the Breed Society.' He was in partnership with H. Dovey and their Lyndhurst ponies were frequently exported as were Mr Dovey's Warren ponies.'

Kay Bailey, January 2005, on Don's retirement from the council.

10

PONY PERSONALITIES

THE COUNCIL OF THE PONY SOCIETY CHOSE A PONY PERSONALITY to go in the Annual Report every year for some fifty years. On the whole show winners were not chosen, they were well known and advertised themselves. Only a very few ponies can win championships and no breeder can breed many champions but they can hope that every pony they breed will have the conformation, temperament and action to do a useful job comfortably. These chosen ponies show how varied these jobs can be. All these accounts were written by their owners. On asking for contributions to a millennium collection, some recollections came out.

WOMAN WHO KEPT THE HOME FIRES BURNING
The first stirrings of genuine sex equality were felt during the Great War when millions of young men went off to fight – leaving women to fill the breach.

Southborough's first bread roundswoman, Miss Ralph, is pictured above with her pony Bob near Christchurch in 1915. She was employed by the bakers Paine-Smith and Co who took over Mules and Co a few years previously – although clearly the company had not got round to changing the sign on the cart by the time this picture was taken.

George Paine, 82, son of George Paine senior, who owned the well known bakery, remembered Miss Ralph well as 'a wonderful little woman' who used to give the occasional ride in her cart. She was the only cart-driver among the women recruited by the company during the war – the rest had to use specially designed hand-barrows, he recalled. Unlike many women workers, Miss Ralph kept her job when the war ended and went on to become manageress of the Paine-Smith restaurant in Monson Road, Tunbridge Wells.

As for her pony, Bob was one of the New Forest ponies regularly driven through Southborough, half broken, to be sold at market. George Paine remembers a particular spot which used to hold a special horror for the little pony.

'A nasty carter once gave Bob a whipping just by the drinking

Bob and Mrs Ralph.

fountain by Skinners School,' he said. 'It was the first whipping he had ever had and from then on he used to bolt when he neared the fountain. Many's the hair-raising ride we used to have trying to bring him under control as he raced along the road.'

Pony personalities from the early days:

Bucklers Golden Farthing, chestnut gelding, 11.3hh, was 2nd in the open under 12.0hh at Olympia in 1934. During the New Year he pulled a governess cart and was one of Princess Alexandra's favourite ponies when she was taught to ride at Holyport by Horace and Sybil Smith.

Monkshorn Candy. Mrs Kermack bought Candy, bay gelding by Monkshorn Danny ex Forest mare, breeder W. House, for her elder daughter. He competed in many spheres and was a brilliant performer. Both Mrs Kermack and her daughter hunted him. He was one in a million.

Cadogan Joan,12.3hh, brown mare, rider Myrtle Rodocamach at Sam Marsh's yard 1941. She was an excellent jumper and won 13.2hh jumping at Royal Richmond Show 1932; she hated rain and could be difficult to catch but taught me a lot and lived well into her twenties.

Sprattsdown Lucille. K. MacSween bought her from her breeder as a yearling; she spent the next 22 years with her. She lived first near Portsmouth then moved up to the Pennines, Lancashire; Scotland, East Yorks and finally back to the Forest. She was honest, willing and adaptable, being broken to harness when 10; she took to it like a duck to water. During the summer there was an endless stream of passengers, these were fun times. The northerners were surprised and impressed with this pint-sized pony that could keep up with their 16.0hh giants with no trouble at all. Lucy did her bit fund raising at the village fete every year giving pony rides. The *East Yorkshire Gazette* printed a photo of her aged 21 when she won the most sporting trophy at Ryehill Show where she carried Leah MacSween aged 3 in the musical blocks, Sam Panton in the walk, trot and run (he was 4 years old), Kirsty MacSween (aged 7) in the egg and spoon and bending, and Samantha Coxwall (aged 9) in the walk and trot and the sack race

Bucklers Golden Farthing.

Warren Peggy.

WARREN PEGGY

Foaled: 1944
Breeder: Mr Fred Smith, of Norley Wood
Owner: Mr H.C. Dovey, of Culverley Farm, Beaulieu
'Warren Peggy is a bay mare of 13.2 hands, owned by Mr H.C. Dovey, of Culverley Farm, Beaulieu. She was bred by Mr Fred Smith, of Norley Wood, in 1944. At an early age she took to trespassing on Mr Dovey's Warren Farm. When barred from other access, she even swam out in the Solent in order to get round the shore fence. Mr Dovey, feeling that it is better to support your own animals rather than those of your neighbours, bought her.

'Peggy had been broken to saddle and harness by her breeder, and she has proved a most versatile and game mare, with a great love of pony and cattle driving. She seems to foresee every move of the driven animals, bringing herself into the right position without any help from her rider. After a successful day's round-up, if the lorry is too full to get Warren Peggy aboard, she can be stripped of her gear and turned loose. Wherever she may be in the Forest, she will set off for home and within twenty-four hours will be back at Warren Farm.

'During the course of her active life Peggy has found time to breed at least ten foals, and it is on her that Mr Dovey's four sons have all learnt to ride. She always, by some uncanny instinct, knows when she has a learner up. In gymkhana and Forest point-to-points she has had considerable success.

'Now at 18 years of age, the mare is as game and strong as ever, and still has all her zest for life.'

WARREN BRISCOE
NPS Vol 26
Foaled: 1948
Sire: Denny Danny
Dam: Forest mare
Breeder: H.C. Dovey
Owner: E. Dovey

'Briscoe was born on the Forest in 1948; his mother was an extremely wild mare who had never been caught since she was a foal. That summer she was caught off-guard grazing with Briscoe on Woodfidley Bridge by Don Stephens who happened to be passing and was able to creep up on her.

'Briscoe was broken as a three-year-old and ran in his first point-to-point that year, coming 2nd in the Children's Race to Mr Andrew's famous Nosey Boy. During the next year he was used colt hunting, cattle drifting and racing. Proving himself to have all his mother's speed, he won the point-to-point Children's Race, ridden by (agister) Brian Ingram. He won many pony races, running in the point-to-point nearly every year for fifteen years and winning twice more. But his young riders were often unseated and his owner spent many a Boxing Day afternoon searching and then trying to catch him on the open Forest.

'He has only been in the show ring three times in his life: twice jumping, when he was sadly eliminated at the very last fence, and once in the Veterans Class, Burley 1972, when he was 7th. He enjoyed every minute of this, being sure he was in the parade paddock and the race would begin any moment.

'Although he has been domesticated and handled since a foal he still at times likes to pretend he has never seen a human being before and can be impossible to catch even in a small field. He has to be cornered, the corner however has to have high sides as he will jump a five bar gate quite easily and disappear snorting and bucking across the next field. Although the years have crept up on him and his wind is not what it was he still enjoys the odd day colt hunting or cattle-drifting, pulling and dancing like a three-year-old. At 25 he enjoys a gallop far too much to be a suitable child's pony. His owner may still be seen using him to check cattle and ponies on the Forest as he loves being taken out.'

ROBIN

Foaled: 1939
Sire: New Forest pony
Dam: The Lady, a New Forest pony
Owner: Mrs P. Seaton Satedham
His owner's account illustrates how by careful training of an ordinary Forest pony can compete successfully in open dressage tests.

'In the autumn of 1944 we bought Robin, a five-year-old bay stallion, at the Beaulieu Road sales. About 13 hands, and very strongly built, he was bred by Mr B. Watts of Burley, who was selling him because of his habit of jumping into fields and gardens. A habit he retains to this day, only in reverse. He regularly jumps out of his field about three o'clock each afternoon unless he is brought in at that time.

'He proved the easiest of ponies to break in. He began by being lunged, a proceeding he considered to be exceedingly boring. A few days later he was led out to graze and after first leaning on him and then lying across his back, I finally got up and rode him home in a halter, and that was the end of his "breaking in".

'He was gelded in the spring of 1945 and led an uneventful life that year.

'In 1946 he came to Gunville and he distinguished himself in the first five minutes by jumping his stable door, which is 4 foot 6 in high. He went to his first shows and won a few prizes in all kinds of events. It was an important year for him as he was nearly ruined by having his head "nagged" into position with a pelham bit. He hunted all that winter with the Portman hounds and went like a bomb, getting much too excited.

'In 1947 he paid the price of bad schooling and used to get over-bent with the result that he won very few prizes that summer. His re-schooling began that autumn and very slowly his manners and carriage improved. He had another season's hunting which he enjoyed and this time he was reasonably quiet.

'In 1948 his schooling began to pay dividends. His action and carriage had improved so much that he came 2nd in the ridden class at the National Pony Show. He ended the show season by winning at Romsey, and it was here that the idea of training him for competitive dressage was thought of. After his ride on him the judge said, "He goes like a dressage horse!" That winter he ran well in the point-to-point races considering his jockey did not know that part of the Forest. His intelligence played him an unlucky trick. Coming to the finish, he heard me cheering him on and, disregarding his jockey, ran out and came to me. Of course by the time he got started again it was too late and he finished fourth. Nevertheless he had proved he was not just a useless show pony.

'In 1949 he did reasonably well in his showing classes, but his most exciting day was his first dressage test. This was at Portbury. He behaved with considerably more calm than his mistress and came 4th. He was the only pony and his marks were not far behind such horses as Carifryn and Conquistador (the champion dressage horse of 1951). He then won the best trained pony test at Burley Show. Came 4th at Camberley and finally in the dressage championships at Henley he was 3rd in the novice test and 5th in the medium test. He was the only pony competing but being a true native pony he did his best and his determined character enabled him to hold his own with the bigger and more elegant horses.

'In 1950 after many years of ups and downs in showing classes he finally succeeded in winning the championship for ridden New Forest ponies at Burley Show, he also won the trained pony test again. He won and was placed in several open dressage tests but his best achievements were a 2nd to Mrs V.D.S. Williams's Clogheen at Camberley and a 4th at the dressage championships.'

LEYGREEN SANDY

No. 2290
Foaled: 1938
Sire: Forest horse
Dam: Orphan II
Breeder: Mr W.H. Penny of Leygreen Farm, Beaulieu
'Sandy was out of No 6505 Orphan II, a 12.2 hand, red roan registered New Forest mare, his sire an unknown Forest stallion.

'Shown by Mr Penny at the stallion show next year, he was awarded the cup for the best yearling; each successive year (except 1942) till he was five years old, he was champion pony of his age and class and also won the National Pony Society Medal for best pony of riding type.

'Spotted by the keen eye of Mrs Glenda Spooner, his valuable services to our breed were abruptly terminated by her having him gelded. Next

Leygreen Sandy.

year, 1944, in the ownership of Miss Muriel Spacey, he commenced his equally successful career as a riding pony. Though standing only 13.1 hands, he won the open 14.2 hand class at Aldershot; this was followed by three further 1sts at the August Show, including Childs Hunter class, which he has won each year ever since.

'1946 saw him carry off top honours in open and breed classes at Hilsea; 1947 at Totton, Fordingbridge, Romsey, Salisbury, Highcliffe and at the Quorn Hunt Pony Club Show in Leicestershire.

'Next year his most important victory was at the National Pony Society's Show at Roehampton, where he not only won the N.F. riding class but was reserve champion riding pony of all Mountain and Moorland breeds. His activities were not, however, confined to the show ring; he carried off the 2nd prize in the jumping class at our August Show; and he also ran in our point-to-point races on Boxing Day.

'On her marriage in 1950, Miss Spacey sold Sandy, who had won over 200 rosettes for her, to Miss Jeanette Coombes of Leigh Farm, Wimborne; in May of that year, he gave his new owner intense pleasure by being placed 2nd in a very large in-hand class of Mountain and

Moorland ponies at the Windsor Show. As a matter of fact he never shows himself to full advantage in-hand, it is his action under saddle that is so outstanding.

'In 1951 he again won the same class at Roehampton; in the two years he has been in Miss Coombes's possession, he has earned 55 rosettes. Miss Coombes says that he goes equally happily in either saddle and with double bridle or halter when at home. His favourite specialities are a bottle of stout and chocolate biscuits, given when he particularly distinguishes himself.

'It is doubtful whether any other pony has been such a good advertisement to our breed and we are indeed grateful to his owners for having brought him so much before the public eye. '

SANDY

Foaled: 1937
Sire: the late Telegraph Rocketer
Dam: unregistered Forest mare.
Breeder: Arthur Taylor of Turf Croft, Burley
Owner: agister R.G. Stickland of Linwood.
'Chestnut gelding, who spent the first two years of his life in and around Harvest Slade. Then the dam with her foal and Sandy arrived at Crow Farm to be impounded by Mr Harry Wright. Mr A. Taylor sold the three for a mere £7 10s. 0d. to Mr H.G. Stickland of Linwood; that was Sandy's lucky day for the wholesale killing of ponies for the meat trade had started locally.

'The halter breaking of Sandy began at once but through not having his halter in its proper position, he all but dislocated his neck. After a good rest, the remainder of his education was undertaken and he proved to be a most versatile and game horse. During his long, hard working life he has never been lame and developed a great love for hunting. A run with hounds delights him, but his uncanny instinct, when colt hunting, to foresee the colt's next move could easily unseat his rider for he has often turned or stopped before you are aware of it. In harness and on the holding, no job puts him out nor is there any that he cannot do.

'On many occasions he has been raced, shining most in the Boxing Day point-to-point. He ran in this event six times, winning once and being placed on four occasions. At Burley this year, he was second in a very strongly contested utility class.

'Sandy is now 20 years old and still going strong.'

Mustang.

MUSTANG
Foaled: 1945
Dam: Ocknell Rosebud
Sire: Forest horse
Breeder: Gerald Forward
Owner: Mrs J. Spring
Mustang is a bright bay standing 12.2 hands.

'I bought him as an entire in October 1949 at Beaulieu Road ... He is a completely self-possessed pony, loving no one really, but himself and his food. He adores a good day's hunting and will gallop and jump all day with the biggest and best horses. He puts up with showing, doing what he is told up to a point. He is the complete and perfect traveller having done a good many miles in our trailer to and from shows and hunting ...

'We did not show Mustang until August 1950. Amongst his winnings was a 1st at Burley in the small ridden class and a 2nd in the best trained NF pony class. First at Lymington in the 12.2 class. First at Bishops Waltham in the 13.2 class and 1st at Bognor Regis 12.2 class.

'In 1951 we showed him rather more both in open and NF classes. At Worthing and Brighton he was second to that lovely little pony Donna. At the Royal Counties, Southampton, he won the big riding class and was reserve champion to Miss O. Burry's Dolly Grey ... At Burley he won the best trained NF pony class ...

'In 1952 Mustang seemed to come in from his winter holiday looking and going better than ever; but as greedy as ever. The Hambledon Pony Club ran a one-day event in the Easter holidays. Mustang was second to a 15.3 hand hunter ... At Henfield, Sussex, he won the British Show Pony Society's Challenge Cup, given for the 13 hand South of England Championship. His other first prizes were at Wellow, Show of the Year Southampton, Burley, NF Agricultural Society's Show and Aldershot... We decided to go to Roehampton this year to try our luck as the pony was going so well. He never seems to be quite the same when he gets near London. He had a real pop in him when he came out of the trailer. However, after a gallop his sanity was restored. He won the NF ridden class and was reserve champion with Criban Heather Bell, a Welsh pony, to another famous Welsh pony Coed Coch Powys for the best Mountain and Moorland Riding Pony. The judges just could not make up their minds and kept sending these ponies out to gallop round the ring. It was a most nerve wracking experience.'

'In the accompanying photograph Mustang's rider is his small future owner, Judy. He will probably be able to teach her far more about riding, hunting and showing, when she is old enough than any person qualified to do so.' The Spring family moved to Ireland, taking Mustang with them.

LUCKY JOE

Foaled: 1923

Owner: Mrs B. Loader

'The property of Mrs B. Loader of the Foresters Arms, Frogham, Fordingbridge, Lucky Joe was born in September 1923. He was such a small weak little foal that Mr Loader said he would not keep him. However, Mrs Loader came to the rescue and gave her husband £1 for the colt.

'He grew well and for the first four years of his life he ran in the Forest, winning his premiums each year at the Stallion Show. When he was four years old he blotted his copybook by killing a foal, so he was taken off the Forest, gelded and broken to ride.

'Mrs Loader used Joe for twenty-two years in her riding stables and he was never sick or sorry. He turned into a wonderful ride, very fast, and his owner says he threw her off more times than any other horse or pony she has ever ridden. Both Mr and Mrs Loader hunted

Lucky Joe, aged 39, with the 3rd generation of the Loader family to ride him.

the pony regularly, and on one occasion in a fast gallop over Ocknell Plain, Joe galloped right past the late Sir George Thursby (then Master of the Buckhounds) on his hunter. When she finally pulled him up at the gate of the enclosure, Mrs Loader apologised to the Master, who merely commented on what a game pony little Joe must be.

'Now in honourable retirement, Lucky Joe gives gentle rides round the orchard to Mr and Mrs Loader's grandchildren. He is a much loved member of the family, and is entering his fortieth year looking fitter than many much younger ponies.'

JOHNNY

Foaled: 1939

'Johnny must be the most versatile New Forest Pony. Standing 13.2 hands, he is a bright bay, foaled in 1939 on the Forest, out of Mr Bob Houses's strawberry roan mare Monkshorn Roan by an unknown New Forest stallion. He is a perfect harness pony, working all the year round on the farm, ploughing, harrowing, pulling logs and carting the hay. He has also won in driving classes. He showed great courage and stamina by winning the open New Forest point-to-point three times in succession, and showed great speed by winning races at the local shows including the scurry at Burley, which he won several times.

'He won over 80 rosettes at gymkhanas and in 1954 he took to polo at Rhinefield without any schooling, with great success. He is very gentle and affectionate, is loved by all children, his patient, quiet manner gives confidence to all he teaches to ride. He enjoys dressing up and is ridden side saddle at carnivals.

'Johnny won several prizes for show jumping but preferred natural jumps. He was a brilliant hunter, hunted two seasons with the Portman hounds, jumping fences higher than himself, and went over many gates. Often he was amongst few to finish after gruelling runs of eight or more miles, having given many hunters a lead over tricky jumps, often he covered thirty miles in a day's hunting, coming home as gay as when he went out.

'He once competed in a cross country event, and was 2nd amongst forty-seven entries. He is a great character, and seems to get younger even as he grows older.
'

MUDEFORD STREAK

NPS 2655   Canadian pony society 14
Sire: Brookside David
Dam: Mudeford Grey Girl foaled 1946
Owners: D.R. and J.G. Mrs Holbrook RR3 Dundas, Ontario, Canada
Breeder: A.E. Burry, Balmer Lawn, Brockenhurst
'Streak won premiums at the stallion show every year from 1 to 5 years old, taking the cup for the best of his age at 2,3 and 4 years. He was sold as a 5-year-old to Ralph Mist, who stood him at stud where among other good ponies he sired the premium winning stallion Corra Tanty. He also put on circus acts with him; he still does several tricks such as giving kisses, shaking hands, counting and has been trained to work in vaulting harness. Mr Mist took Streak with him to Canada and there sold him to Mrs Holbrook. His marvellous manners and ability have made it possible for him to compete in performance classes in Canada where stallions are rarely shown under tack. He was hunted with the Hamilton Hunt, a recognised hunt in Ontario, shown in Working Pony classes, Pony Jumper and in hand classes where he has won championships, reserve championships and best of breed. He was ridden in the C team of the Hamilton Hunt Pony Club at the National Pony Club rally at London, Ontario, in 1961 by a 13-year-old girl and also took part in the branch display dressed up as a clown. He was 2nd in the cross country individual standing. Now retired to stud he has sired more than 25 ponies in Canada and is still going strong and looking wonderful.

His beautiful disposition has carried on to his get and there became more demand for New Forest ponies in Canada as a result.'

TANNER
NPS3081
Sire: Titmouse
Dam: Shobley Augusta
Breeder: Sir Berkeley Pigott
Owner: Miss P. V. Mangin

'Tanner was bought from Sir Berkeley Pigott when he was three months old by his present owner Miss P. V. Mangin. His mother Shobley Augusta was a daughter of Sir Berkeley's famous Lady Roe. His father, Titmouse, was a direct descendant of the late Miss Jackson's well known Brookside ponies. He ran on the Forest until he was three years old, except for a short time while recovering from a road accident in which one hind leg was badly damaged and he was also suffering from a severe type of poisoning. He looked so miserable that he was rather unkindly christened Dopey. A name by which he is known to many friends today.

'He was broken in shortly afterwards and one member of the Forest community remembers his bucking to this day and the sore legs

Pennyfarthing and Tanner.

which he had as a result. His buck is no pretence, and being rather short in front, he can be very difficult to stay on. His main occupation was intended to be polo, but after two seasons, he was declared by some people to be dangerous to players owing to his unpredictable behaviour.

'He started his racing career by chance. He was being ridden peacefully near East Boldre when a voice was heard to say, "That pony will never win a race at Burley." So he was entered just to see. Since then he ran in seventeen races with sixteen wins and one 2nd. He also won many other races, and he was never less than 2nd. He has also won many other races, and I cannot remember him ever being less than second. Besides these shorter races, he has won the Point-to-Point four times in the Open New Forest Pony Race. He always lives out and has little regular exercise.'

BLACK RIBOT
NFS 977
Sire: Ribot
Dam: Coppice Phyllida
Breeder: Miss A.M. Shead
Owner: Mr I.C. Jewell, Reading
'Purchased by Mr I.C. Jewell, Reading, at Beaulieu Road in 1959 for £15 15s. 0d. Mr Jewell's daughter Marilyn, with the aid of her grandfather, broke and trained the pony herself, and he grew to be just over 14 hands. In 1965 he was registered with the BSJA and in one season he was upgraded JA and won over 50 cups and trophies, 500 rosettes and £500 in prize money show jumping. In 1967 his winnings included The Royal Windsor Junior Championship, Bishops Waltham Agriculture Show, Romsey Show, National Pony Club Championship at Hickstead and numerous other prizes. As Marilyn still has two seasons to jump in junior events, they hope to qualify for the leading Junior Show Jumper of the Year at the Horse of the Year Show. This record is a fine achievement for a New Forest pony which cost 15 guineas and is now valued at £1,500.'

BEACON BRIAR
NPS3678
Foaled: 1955
Sire: Newtown Spark
Dam: Beacon Bramble
Brown stallion

'Briar's first public appearance was in the Burley Carnival, aged eight weeks, with a paper ruff round his neck and an enormous blue silk sash round his middle. As a foal he accompanied his mother, puppylike, on rides every day from August. He attended Pony Club rallies, including trotting behind her over to the Pony Club gymkhana, a distance of fourteen miles there and back. He won a foal premium at Burley and after being 2nd at the stallion show as a yearling, was turned on the Forest. He ran until the following March and was 3rd in the two-year-old class in April. That autumn we collected him from some Ringwood gardens, and were surprised to be told that the children would miss him! Not the usual reception collectors of lane creepers received!

'Having got him home, we broke him in and he spent the winter with Beacon Julian who is a year younger. He gained a £10 premium as a three-year-old and ran out all summer. That winter he was introduced to hunting and went out regularly afterwards. He was also 3rd in the novice race at the point-to-point.

'In April he was reserve for the four-year-old cup and was turned out on Durrhill where he had a three-day running battle with Julian, officially allocated to Longcross! During this battle Briar chased Julian across Thorney Hill railway bridge and was knocked over by a car. Fortunately only grazed, he must have thought Julian had done it, as, although always ready to get his own back on Julian, he was not made traffic shy. The following year he was again reserve in the five-year-old class to the cup winner.

'From then on this most versatile pony has never missed his turn, whether it has been hunting, colt hunting, riding school work, jumping, racing, gymkhanas or running on the Forest with his mares. Except for once pulling a ligament in a rabbit hole he has never been lame or sick.

'He has frequently carried over ten stone for seven hours hunting, comes home, eats up and is ready to do two hours in the school next day. He is marvellous in the school, as he is a perfect gentleman, quiet for a child and yet strong and comfortable for an adult. Having 9 in. of bone and yet being narrow, he can take all sizes. He must have been one of the most regular attenders of Burley Group Pony Club rallies. Numerous children have taken C Test on him, and, since he adores attention, he is usually used to practise bandaging. One child to each leg and a fifth trying to get round his very full and slippery tail. His mane being about two feet long lends itself to plaiting in fancy but not orthodox styles and has kept many children happy for hours. He can be left with the smallest child in a milling collecting ring at a gymkhana

Beacon Briar.

and is always tied up next to other ponies. A short summary of some of his wins in 1963 shows his versatility:

'1963: 3rd ridden stallion Mountain and Moorland class, Ponies of Britain; Reserve for Shobley Cup at our stallion show; 2nd open race, point-to-point.'

SURPRISE V
NPS6194
Foaled: 1936
Owner and breeder: Mrs Mackworth Praed
Sire: Forest horse
Dam: Snowball II
'Surprise got her name as the mare Snowball recently bought was not supposed to be in foal and had been hunted all the Easter holidays by her small owner. While still a sucker Surprise staked herself badly, luckily the big three-cornered tear in her chest was hardly more than skin deep and soon healed and her roan coat turned grey and then white, the scar became barely visible. She was broken to ride and drive and, during the war, was lent to Sir George Lowndes of Crow, who drove her in a four-wheeled buggy. Returning to Castletop, she was

Surprise V, 1958, aged 22.

highly commended with her mother as a pair in the driving class at the Burley Show, 1947, her only appearance in the show ring, though she was entered once in the children's race at the same show but not placed - possibly due to her rider not noticing the race had started! She won the prize for the "pony with the prettiest head" at a Pony Club gymkhana, has attended their camp and innumerable rallies. With another Forest pony she drew Boadicea's chariot in the 1953 Pony Club pageant, but her great joy is hunting, and she is well known with the New Forest Buckhounds, having carried three generations of her owner's family besides many others - grown-ups and children. She played polo at Rhinefield, was in the winning team for the Holly Hill cup in 1954 and in the Pony Club team when the New Forest Hunts Branch played Paddock Polo at Roehampton in 1955. Aged 22, she was in the winning team of the NF Pony Club inter-group competition run on Prince Philip lines.

'In harness, besides being driven in a light trap, she helped with the usual harrowing, carting, etc, of a smallholding, and was even requisitioned to take voters to the poll. In fact, an all-round pony, though barely 12.2 hands.

'She is still an excellent ride, gay and keen, perhaps not a first pony as she prefers to prance along sideways; but when dismounted will stand like a rock till her rider is on again - more or less - when she is off like a rocket and apparently as tireless. Very useful in Musical Logs, a game she thoroughly enjoys.

'Though often turned out on the Forest, she never, sadly, bred.'

LADYBIRD XVII
NPS7883
13.2 hands
Dam: Dolly
Breeder: J. Drodge
Owner: Mrs S. Parker

'Ladybird was born in the New Forest out of a dark brown forest mare called Dolly; her breeder was J. Drodge, of Ivy Cottage, Norley Wood.

'During 1942 Ladybird was the fastest pony colt-hunting in the Forest, ridden by L. Mansbridge. She was also used in harness to collect swill from an army camp. In 1943 she had a beautiful chestnut filly foal with a flaxen mane and tail and white stockings by the Forest stallion Lucky Jim. She then moved to Dorset and in 1947 bred a colt by Blunderbus GSB and a filly by Terry GSB in 1948; in 1951 she had another cross-bred colt but in 1953 she was back to work teaching her owner's children to ride, raking, turning and carting hay, and still able to clear 4 ft 6 in. with ease. She was put to an Arab stallion in 1960 but without result, she continued to be ridden and was as fast and keen as ever up to 1968, since then she has remained fit and happy. She has had the same owner since 1942.'

MR ANDRÉ
NFG 167
Foaled: 1959
Dam: Miranda II
Sire: Marmalade II
Breeder: Creed
Owner: Sandra Noble

'13.2½ hands, dark bay with black points, he now belongs to me, Sandra Noble. Bred in 1959 by the Creed family at Ower Farm, Calshot, he spent his early life at the farm and as a well grown lively two-year-old was broken in by our local agister, Brian Ingram.

'My family have known André since he was two but weren't in a position to buy him when, at about the age of three or four, he was eventually sold to the Pleydell-Bouveries. He proved to be rather a handful for his new owner so was sent to a nearby riding stables to be "quietened down". In 1964, during his period at the stables, Dad rode him in the Boxing Day point-to-point, and although straight out of the field, with no extra food and carrying considerably more weight than he should have been, he came in fourth. Dad was impressed with his performance and became determined that we should own him. He was in the stables for a few more years when we heard he was going to be sold; we weren't going to let the chance of buying him slip away again, so in August 1967 Mr André became a member of the Ralphs' establishment.

'What an awkward, pig-headed little "b" he had turned into. I really had my work cut out making something of him. I rode him mostly but my sister, Veida, sometimes jumped him, and brother Michael was André's racing jockey. As a combination they did extremely well in the local pony races and at his peak André was unbeatable in any Forest Pony race, winning the Tanner Cup three years running in 1968, 1969 and 1970.

'Dad gave me André as my 21st birthday present and we have competed in almost every aspect of competitive and non-competitive riding. Between us we have won hundreds of rosettes and numerous cups and awards for various events including gymkhana, jumping, handy hunter, hunter trials, point-to-point, pony racing, pony club events, barrel racing and showing, to name but a few, showing André's versatility and adaptability as a good all-round pony for which the Forest breed is renowned.

'Whilst expecting our first baby, André taught husband Bill to ride, and in two years they have competed in pony races and point-to-point twice, coming in 4th and last year 2nd in the Open Forest Pony Race. There is nothing André likes more than galloping around on the Forest and really enjoys the colt-hunting and cattle drifting seasons. Bill has improved considerably at colt-hunting since his first attempt in the summer of 1973 when André got shot of him twice before they even started any colt-hunting.

'To those who know him, André is quite a character; one of his distasteful little tricks however, is lying down in water. Veida and I have both been drenched when André has laid down in streams, and now he is virtually "dared with a big stick" to go down in water.

'Upon reflection, Mr André has given all of us, including Mum who doesn't ride, a great deal of pleasure and enjoyment and perhaps one day if he decides he would like to ride, my young son, Lee, will have as much fun with him as I have been lucky enough to have.'

MERRIE MARTINI

NFM 1015
Foaled: 1961
Sire: Merrie Mercury
Dam: Merrie Martha
Owner and breeder: Susan Shaw
13 hands

'Martini came to the fore as a yearling at the Breed Show, when, much to everyone's surprise, she became overall champion. For the next few years she was lightly shown and then joined the breeding herd. Her best known son was Merrie Mandate, winner of the Performance Pony last year.

'When Sarah Jane (my daughter) was seven, she was in need of a pony and ten-year-old Martini was broken for her and together they formed a great partnership. The same year she won the small novice at the Breed Show and the small open at Romsey. They went on to compete successfully in many competitions, including working pony, family pony, show jumping, gymkhanas and Pony Club events. She spend

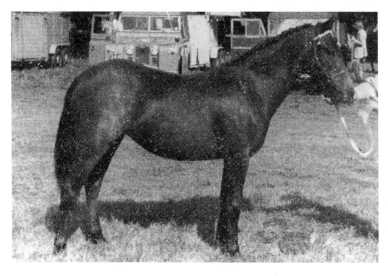

Merrie Martini as a yearling.

five happy years with Sarah Jane, supposedly "retiring" to the riding school with a final fling at the Breed Show in 1975, winning three 1sts and two 2nds in five classes.

'During her "retirement" she taught many children to ride and introduced them to the Pony Club and hunting. She also became an expert cow pony, twisting and turning so quickly after strays that it was difficult to stay with her. Then Richard, aged five, started riding her and she took him safely in the ring off the lead, knowing exactly what to do. In 1980 she returned to the Breed Show and again won the Small Open and was well placed in the working pony and first pony class, by this time aged 19. In 1981 with the height now raised to 13.2, she went back to defend her title and took the cup home for the third time, as well as being 2nd in the working pony.

'Martini continues to be the favourite pony in the riding school. She can be quite naughty with a competent rider, but always behaves perfectly with Richard, whom she takes hunting whenever possible She has been an outstanding pony, capable of excelling in any sphere and proving by her late introduction to riding that ponies are never too old to learn.'

BURNREW RUSSET
NPS 2939
Foaled: 1949
Dam: Deeracres Pippin
Sire: Newtown Spark
Breeder: Captain F.H. Barber
Owner: Jenny Gaitskill

'Bred by Captain F.H. Barber, Russet spent two years running on the Forest as a stallion and was broken in by Capt. Barber's son, Jeremy. After the Stallion Show, when he was five years old, it was decided to geld Russet as the trend was towards the larger more quality show ponies for breeding; although he was a strong, compact little pony, standing 12.3½ by no stretch of the imagination could he be called large or show quality. Whether this trend was such a good idea has been subject of much speculation.

'He was soon bought by his present owner, Jenny Gaitskill, for £50, which included all the tack. The next few years were spent doing the rounds of the local shows, gymkhanas and hunter trials. Always working off grass, he would hack to the shows in the early hours; take part in everything possible on the programme – showing, jumping, racing and gymkhana and hack home again in the evening. He won numerous rosettes which one year included the field sports society rosette for hunting with the buckhounds.

'Taking part in three of the Boxing Day point-to-points, he came 2nd once in spite of having had only four days' exercise as his owner was at boarding school.

'Fifteen years ago, Russet's half brother was bought to take over from Russet, when it was thought he would start to slow down in his early twenties. His owner was obviously being slightly previous as at the age of 31 he has slowed down very little and has no intention of a young upstart of 15 taking over.

'He proved a worthy winner of the 1979 Ridden Veteran Class & Blashford Cup at the Breed Show and still enjoys hunting and – any excuse for a gallop. Perhaps his greatest qualities are his courage, generosity (always finding something extra when needed) and his sure footedness across country (only depositing his owner three times in 26 years!)

'Thank you, Russet - you owe me nothing.'

BULL HILL FANLIGHT
Foaled: 1973
Sire: Knightsbridge Falstaff
Dam: Bull Mill Delight
Breeder: Mrs E. Dunlop
Owner: Miss S. Goodchild

'Bull Hill Fanlight has made a wonderful recovery from a very bad road accident, and, hating to be left out, was entered for some local dressage to see if the judges thought he was going level. He was 4th and 5th first time out, 3rd and 4th second time, 1st and 2nd third time, beating his owner's affiliated horse. He managed to win a Family Pony Championship and Mountain & Moorland Riding Club Championship qualifying on his only appearance. He won the Mountain & Moorland ridden at Orsett agricultural show and was 2nd in-hand at Essex County. He also won a medium unaffiliated dressage class after which he was affiliated as a 'horse' and in December did a Prix St George with credit. Stacy Goodchild had taken her horse to medium standard but needed to learn more herself without "mucking up" the horse, so she had used Fanlight as a guinea pig. Piaffe, pirouettes, passage have been no problem; he is of course hampered by his pony paces and conformation but anyone, not least himself, has a lot of fun. He is much slimmer and fitter now, little does he know how close he came to the bullet.'

MIGHTY MOUSE

by Patricia James

Mighty Mouse

'In 1970 we were looking for a 13.2 hand pony for Sophie who was 11. After looking and trying many, we saw Mighty Mouse advertised in the *Western Gazette*. Early on Saturday morning we went to Beaminster (Dorset) and saw this pony with enormous eyes and very long ears and a hogged mane. The more we looked, the more we liked him and Sophie thought him super – he jumped really well.

'Gradually over the next four months he and Sophie got to know each other well. At some stage he had been very knocked about, you couldn't touch his head. It could take 30 minutes to put on his bridle. If you carried a stick he was off, and to hog him meant using a twitch. Soon we started to take him to Pony Club rallies and local shows and Sophie's collection of rosettes grew rapidly, the colours changing from pink and pale blue to red and royal blue.

'One day at a show, Sophie looked covetously at a huge cup for 14.2 jumping. "You can only enter if you win the 13.2 jumping," I said, thinking, "That's that." Mouse brought home both cups that day. Then, when I took off his saddle, an onlooker noticed his brand and said that was F. Sparks's brand and he was a registered New Forest pony. We learned that he had been foaled on the Forest by Slipper ex Blaze of Thorneycroft. He had been sold at Beaulieu Road sales as a foal to a Scotsman who, when he found it would cost more to transport him to Scotland than he had paid for him, left him in Hampshire. He was gelded and turned on the Forest until backed and sold eventually to Mrs Pym.

'In the Pony Club hunter trials he had two 2nds and one 3rd in classes of 97, 103 and 111 entries. He never came home without a rosette and frequently with many. We went to Peterborough in the days when they only had four WHP classes and he jumped one of three clear rounds from 62 competitors to finish 6th. He was in the Wilton Pony Club, Prince Philip team, and had prizes presented to him by Lord Mountbatten and David Broome. Twice he was 3rd in the New Forest Breed Performance Pony of the Year. Both Sophie and Lucy had the thrill of riding at Olympia at the Christmas Show and hearing Raymond Brookes-Ward making flattering comments about Mouse.

'One summer at a show there was a brood mare and foal class in the adjacent ring. Mouse behaved like a maniac and certainly did NOT win anything. He just wanted to be with the foals. So I borrowed a delightful pony mare and foal from a friend and turned them out next

Mighty Mouse.

to Mouse and his companion. However, each morning when we woke there in one field was this "family" party of Mouse, the mare and foal, all happy and very close. They would frequently lie down in a huddle together. He's always loved foals and gradually has learnt to behave and set them an example rather than continually thinking he was one himself.

'He was invited to the Royal one year to represent the breed on the "breed stand" and take part in the ridden exhibition of Mountain and Moorland ponies. This was great fun. He really enjoyed himself and stood with his head over the box door obligingly eating quantities of ice-cream and candy floss he was offered by the crowds. The next day he was quite off-colour and his kidneys seemed affected, but within two days he had recovered and qualified again for Peterborough.

'Lucy rode him one year in the New Forest point-to-point on Boxing Day, her cross-country colours were purple. We left her and Mouse at Burley for the start and drove on to Wilverley where the finish was. She didn't know that area very well as we live near Fordingbridge. The crowds were very thick at the finish and it was difficult to see. A rider with a white cap flashed by and a long, long, way behind came the rest. We never saw a purple cap and I was starting to worry, when there were Lucy and Mouse untacked and his eyes shining, standing behind us. "Didn't you see us win?" She asked, "He was miles in front, quite brilliant and I'm sorry but I lost my purple silk."

'When 1976 came to an end, Lucy was growing and we felt the time had come to part with him and to let him teach another family all he had taught us. He went all the way to Cumberland to the edge of the Lake District where he was very happy with the Hart family, pony clubbing, in Prince Philip games teams, hunter trialling and show jumping, restoring confidence to their daughters, one of whom had been badly frightened. Like all humans, they grew too, the arrangement had always been that I would buy him back. This I did for a token (although Mr Hart had paid me generously). As he said Mouse was so special no money could really buy him. So Lucy and I drove to the Lake District and brought him home to Hampshire.

'Now about two weeks previously Cherry East-Rigby had said to me she was looking for the perfect 13 hand WHP schoolmaster jumper, safe in traffic and on the Forest, brilliant at cross-country, etc, etc, and did I know where she could find this equine paragon. "Oh yes,"I said, "in Cumberland and he's called Mighty Mouse."

MIGHTY MOUSE PART II

by Cherry East-Rigby

'I shall always remember the first time we looked at Mouse. He did indeed look "mighty", standing at 13 hands, proudly walking free around Patricia James's yard. I did think that he might have been too much for my daughter Tamarisk to manage but as Patricia said and we found out, he really was the perfect nanny. The first Working Hunter Pony Class we tried, he won, having bravely negotiated a huge Jacob's Ladder out of a trot and coming from an impossible angle. He didn't stop because he knew Tamarisk would fall off if he did. That was May 1982 when Mouse was 18 years old. He came to the Society's Breed Show that year, our first visit, and in the Grand Parade, Tamarisk had rosettes all the way round her waist and Mouse looked so proud with his characteristic high tail carriage, when the announcer said, "Welcome back, Mighty Mouse, you really genuine pony."

'For four seasons until the end of 1985 he gained over 80 WHP rosettes reaching the age of 21 years in his last season with the BSPS. He was usually placed and we were thrilled with him because the standard has become so high in these classes and he was competing against ponies so much younger than himself.

'When we first had Mouse we were very new to showing and we were new to the area and it was quite astonishing the effect he had on people. Everywhere we went they would come over to talk to him. One judge actually had tears in her eyes when she saw him again and another quite suddenly gave him a big hug in the middle of judging a class.

'In 1983 Mouse won the Mighty Mouse Cup for 13.2 jumping at the Wilton Pony Club Show. This had been presented by the James family in his memory after Mouse had gone north, never imagining that he would be back as vigorous as ever. He won again this year too.'

BURTON TOSCA

NFM10241
Foaled: 1950
Breeder: Harry Sparks
Sire: Forest Horse
Dam: Forest Pony
Owner: Mrs Witherby

'Humble beginnings for such a superlative pony. Her dam was a grey mare running on the old Holmsley aerodrome and there Tosca began her days and was branded HS.

'In 1953 she was sold at the Beaulieu Road sales to Mr Crabb Burton, a man, as we all know, with a keen eye for a winner. He put her out on his water meadows, having little work for her so, when by chance I told him I was looking for a pony for my eight-year-old daughter, he told me he might have just the one.

'My first introduction to Burton Tosca was when Mr Crabb took me down to his water meadow and, going up to the fattest of the ponies there, neatly landed himself sideways on her accommodating quarters. This demonstration as to suitability was something of a surprise to us both, however Tosca joined in the fun of the moment by doing no worse than walking off with him, so he had to jump down. She then turned her beautiful head with its intelligent and gentle eyes and I was captivated. The snap decision she was the pony for my daughter Jacqueline English was one we never regretted and have felt eternally grateful to Mr Crabb for letting us have her.

'Being young, little ridden and full of the joys of life, she was a bit too quick on occasion for her young owner, shooting her off the other side as fast as she got on in those early gymkhana days. But they soon came to terms and settled to a splendid and successful partnership. Hunting, showing, jumping and gymkhanas she did to her best with great zest and enthusiasm. She won showing championship cups and rosettes in both Open and New Forest classes, jumping prizes in both 13.2 and 12.2 classes and represented the New Forest in the Prince Philip Cup team. She excelled in all she did and even had the honour of being called "the most intelligent pony I have ever known" by the great horseman Phil Blackmore. Jacqueline's proudest moments for Tosca were when at a large show she won the cup for "the best pony of the day for all-round performance".

'Since Jacqueline left home for work I have had years of enjoyment from her. Until she was in her mid twenties I hunted her with the buckhounds and with a bit of corner cutting she was always right there with the hounds. Now, if there is a near meet, we make a point of "running into them" for our mutual thrill when the years drop from her and she behaves like an over-excited youngster, cavorting around until my old bones can stand no more and reluctantly take her home. When Jacqueline comes down for the odd weekend she takes her out for a ride and invariably returns in fits of laughter from the antics Tosca has been up to over some excitement or other.

'Now she is also teaching the grandchildren to ride with whom she shows so much understanding and gentleness. She is so good with them that I have complete trust in her when they go into the stable with her unattended, even though I have caught them short-cutting by way of under her tummy.'

SISTER AND BROTHER
RANDALLS SUNSHINE. 1980. RANDALLS FIRE. 1981

Sire: Slipalong of St Andrews
Dam: Broomy Sylvia
Breeder: Mrs J. Wright
Owner of Sunshine:Vieda Barfoot (mother of Joanne, Jonathan and Kimberley Barfoot)
Owner of Fire: Miss E. Wright
'Below listed are Sunshine's (Faggot's) achievements as far as the children and I can remember! She has been ridden successfully by all three of them on different occasions. She has represented the NF Pony Club in the Junior Show Jumping Team with Jo and Kim, and been ridden by all three in tetrathlon. She has won the point-to-point seven times, 1st in the NF novice over 3 miles before we bought her. She raced over 1½ miles in the Children's Race: two 1sts at Christmas and 1st Easter with Jo and the same ridden by Kim. Her show jumping winnings are numerous, during 1988 she was almost unbeatable in

Randalls Sunshine, Easter 1991 point-to-point.

local shows, winning over 20 cups and trophies, also the Open NF jumping at the Breed Show with Jo, the 11 and under with Kim in 1988 and 1990. (We did not attend in 1991) Faggot was affiliated in 1989 when many shows were cancelled due to the flu virus, but she did qualify by winning 6 newcomers and 2 foxhunters plus several double clears in both to compete in the Regional Final in July 1991. Jo by this time was just too tall and had to have her stirrups hoisted up to avoid her legs knocking the jumps, so Kim rode her at the Regional Finals. Faggot was one of the smallest ponies, being just 13 hands, and most of the others were 14.2; she had 4 faults. So by no means disgraced herself. She has won the Hampshire Jumping Championships in 1989 and 1990. She has won several hunter trials, junior and open with both riders, in the New Forest and Meon Valley. She is never sick or sorry and is truly worth her weight in gold. She is not too keen on men for some reason. She does have a "little madam" personality at times and I suppose that is how she acquired her nickname "Faggot". She does hate being clipped and has to be heavily sedated (large horse dose), she accepts she has to have shoes, but only if the blacksmith does not lift her hooves more than 6" off the ground. She is rather an escapologist where her rugs are concerned and always seems to have tried to get them off at night.

'Ideally she likes being in the field full time although she is "in" at night. Jo and Kim have both hunted her with the NF buckhounds, and

Randalls Fire, Easter 1991 point-to-point.

she doesn't need a key to open gates! She has attended Pony Club camp every year since we had her.

'Fire ran the Forest as a 2,3 and 4 year-old. He won his classes at the stallion shows and 1st class premiums. He was Champion off the Forest, wining the Shobley Cup as a 3-year-old. Unfortunately he bruised his sole just prior to the Stallion Show and was unable to compete as a 4-year-old. He was broken with no trouble. At four he was a member of the musical ride for 2 years, attending the Food and Farming exhibition in Hyde Park. Competed four times in the point-to-point, twice 2nd and two wins. It might be interesting to have a match with his sister. His progeny are doing well in the show ring.'

MERRIE MISS MARPLE

Sire: Merrie Marmalade
Dam: Merrie Maryon
Owner: Ros Daniels
'Merrie Miss Marple, a grey, inherited her jumping ability from her sire, Merrie Marmalade, and her gorgeous looks from her dam, Merrie Maryon. This combination combined with a very affectionate temperament, endeared her to Mary Godon-Watson, who used her in her publication *Learn to Ride in a Weekend*. She is a Champion in both in-hand and ridden Mountain and Moorland classes and has won

(partnered by her owner Ros Daniels) dressage, show-jumping, cross country, working hunter pony and various other classes. Ros still finds time to drive her little exercise cart round the lanes and Peter Munt, who broke her to harness, predicted a great future for her in private drive. Unfortunately time and money did not permit this extra very time-consuming activity.

'She was New Forest representative at the ASDA festival of farming in Hyde Park, London. Breed representatives came from all over the country, many of them very well known ponies, but Mattie, who is a terrible show-off, gave them all a run for their money, sometimes even rivalling the Section D stallion for presence! Additionally, on arrival I was informed the police horse demonstrating road safety was unavailable and Mattie was asked to take his place. She seemed to understand this was not showing and performed twice a day for four days without putting a hoof wrong – which was probably a relief for H.R. Owen, who had supplied a brand-new Discovery car to 'perform' in the ring with us. Certain members of other breed societies waited with bated breath for hoof marks on the car. They were unlucky!

'Taking part in this festival was an unforgettable experience - I am sure it will be a long time before the pony and I forget the experience of crowds, five deep in front of her stable, with children climbing up the

Merrie Miss Marple.

Ashfield Black Jack, 1997.

bars to get at her! She soon acquired the knack of retreating to the back of the stable and watching the animals perform in front of her! Having spent five days there with five performances a day, we both had a well deserved rest on returning home and are now going to concentrate on dressage and combined training.'

ASHFIELD BLACK JACK

by Laura Wilson

'We bought Ashfield Black Jack as a four-year-old from Barbara Stiles who bought him from Jack's breeder, Mr R.G. Ralphs. Jack's sire is Willoway Piper's Gold and his dam Ashfield Bunty. He was destined initially to become a PC tetrathlon team member alongside brother Piers, who became too tall. So Jack continued his fifth year with myself doing a few shows, dressage, ODE and some much loved hunting. In 1996 he started his first full season showing, which culminated in a 5th and top New Forest at Wembley and his Olympia debut. In 1997 he had many triumphs, starting with three out of five Wembley semi-final qualifiers, PUK WHP, ridden and RC qualifiers, numerous championships and supremes. His most notable wins last year were at the NF county show, where he took both the NF ridden championship and the Mountain and Moorland WHP championship. He took part in the President's challenge and also managed to include a morning's cubbing with the New Forest foxhounds thanks to Mrs Dixon at Minstead. Another important win was the Dalkeith Junior ridden championship at PUK, a first for the breed. In October, at the Horse of the Year Show he won the final of the NPS Mountain and Moorland WHP championship, enabling me to fulfil a lifelong ambition and finishing off a very special season.

'This is the third success for the breed in this championship. Previous winners are: Matins, owned by Roselle Bonney and Merrie Marmalade owned by Susan Shaw of the Merrie Stud.'

DEWLANDS VAL DOONICAN

Foaled: 1980
Breeder: Ann Parry
Owner: Mrs Mary Bryant
The grey, 16-year-old New Forest stallion fresh from his triumphs in the show ring and his appearance with the Horse and Hound New Forest enthusiasts musical ride in Hyde Park, appeared at the press launch

Dewlands Val Doonican.

'Pegasus audition' on summer solstice day in the middle of the New Forest. This grand stallion accepting the great white wings without hesitation, made his appearance at the New Forest and Hampshire County Show, representing Pegasus, the white winged horse of dreams at the launch of a new activity book, *My Pegasus Book of Dreams and Ambitions*.

He appeared on BBC South Today and in many of the local papers, showing in every way the ability, temperament and versatility of the New Forest breed.

CANTERTON BEAU (KNOWN AS BILL)

Foaled: 1994
Sire: Bakeburn Romeo
Dam: Canterton Brownie
Owner: Caroline Wilkins

'What is special about Canterton Beau is that he is a Forest bred pony and he has that lovely Forest look, bright-eyed, bright bay, with a cheeky cheery presence, which catches spectators and the judge's eye as he competes and performs in displays around the country. He will never make the top of any one discipline, but he will try his best and enjoy all asked of him by his enthusiastic rider, Caroline Wilkins.

'Caroline and Bill began the year hunting. First time out he was so sensible he got the job of gate shutter. Next came NFPEC junior indoor show jumping team. He jumped a double clear for the team at Hartpury in the finals. He then competed for the Goodwood Pony Club show jumping and event teams. After competing in the invitation classes at Windsor Horse Trials, Caroline introduced the crowds to the pleasures of riding New Forest ponies side saddle for the NF pony publicity group. Then in a severe rainstorm he teamed up with Jane Holderness-Roddam for a clear round in the eventers challenge.

'The CLA game fair at Broadlands was a wonderful occasion where he joined the display team with two other Forest-bred ponies, Bakeburn Starman, ridden by Beth Robertson, and Trenley Pacific Adventure, ridden by Olivia Sims. Venture was to become his particular friend; they met and competed together at occasions such as the Knightwood Challenge where Venture came 3rd. Bill had a steady clear, not quite fast enough but like his sire, Bakeburn Romeo, speed comes with time and experience. With so many competitions a ride and fish and chips on a beach near us was a favourite outing. He preferred licking breakwaters to chips! Bill was an ideal assistant for Caroline with her

Canterton Beau

carefully chosen GCSE Geography investigation of local bridleways. For Caroline and Bill to travel to Holland for the Dutch National Side saddle championships, the complicated paperwork needed an A level to understand it. Luckily once there, everyone spoke English. Bill was a bit lazy in the midday sun and so Caroline's father tried to make excuses for him by pointing out that he had never been abroad before. He performed well in the afternoon to be 4th in the period costume dressage to music. The whole experience was fantastic and Caroline hopes to take Bill to the French National Championships next year.

'Although only 5th in UK National Side-Saddle Show Pas Seule dressage to music in their Mary Queen of Scots costume with early Flemish music, this was an excellent result for the pair with only dressage horses and adults above him. He hears the music and rises to the occasion. On another occasion Caroline teamed with Olivia Sims and their delightful performance of Bill and Ben in costume won 3rd place again in a very strong class of horses at the National SS Pas de Deux competition.

'Bill is very used to staying in different temporary stables but a problem has arisen: once having found grass under shavings he always digs his bed up just in case there is grass underneath. At HOYS he only found the NEC car park and in Dover, where the stables had about three-foot deep litter, he nearly got to Australia.

'Despite this extremely busy year, Bill has found time to be a great inspiration to his two young RDA riders in John Lasseter's new indoor school. He has become an ideal pony for young riders who are keen to learn rising trot, as the irregular bumping does not bother him. He has also learnt that when his over-keen rider shouts, "Trot on, trot on, trot on" before starting he must wait for his helpers to be ready as the rest of the riders may be only just getting on. He always knows which helpers have carrots, polos and apples in their pockets and subtly sidles up to them whenever possible.

'Now the highlights of the year, 2nd in the junior side saddle Concours d'Elegance. A competition to find the most elegant overall side-saddle picture. Bill and Caroline looked stunning beaten only by a rider on a show horse. The thrill of clearing 3'6" side-saddle in a Chase-me-Charlie, galloping alongside the huntsman at a pony club meet, being a member of the NFPEC indoor team and finally the jumping display at the Horse of the Year Show for the Side-Saddle Association. "Caroline Wilkins riding her New Forest pony Canterton Beau" was announced to the crowds.

'Canterton Beau is a pony personality but he is not unique.

Caroline had as much success with her first Forest-bred pony Tiptoe Bracken II. A keen rider and a Forest-bred pony are a fantastic combination. There are many Forest-bred ponies like Bill and Bracken in the country all capable of doing what Bill has done this year. They love their work but remember they are often late to mature and need variety of work, love and most of all ... understanding.'

WILLOWAY HIGHLAND MALT

Sire: Willoway Pipers Gold
Dam: Mannington Brandy
Owner: Rae Turner

'2001 was a bad year that just got worse, with foot and mouth disease and the restrictions; living just 6 miles from Longtown it just spread out like ripples on a pool with very few farms unaffected. Ourselves, we lost our sheep in the cull. But silently the horse world suffered – no hunting, shows, hunter trials, point-to-points, endurance, even the three equestrian centres in the Carlisle area eventually closed. In fact I saw no point in keeping the ponies shod.

'At the beginning of June the equestrian centres opened up again because of needed revenue. So indoor jumping and unaffiliated dressage started again, with no help from MAFF-DEFRA, who tried to stop them with their stupid rules, but it got started.

'So I started unaffiliated dressage with my stallion, W.H. Malt. As he had a year and a half off work, due to my illness, he had a holiday with Miranda Wallace in Devon. Malt had not forgotten his early schooling. So his first test, a prelim 2, was won. With a points system running from June to September, Malt won five more times, so headed the points and won the summer points Preliminary Trophy. His percentages were just getting better through the '60s into the '70s. So into the winter Points championship with a lot to live up to. Our biggest rival is a registered Fell pony.

'Before Malt went to Cumbria in 1999 he had started riding and was beginning to excel at it. I was finding he could trot at 7 mph and so eat up the miles. His heart rate before and after rides was very good. In the first year he did just 6 pleasure rides of under 20 miles under the Scottish Endurance Riding Club Rules, accumulating 89 miles just short of the magic 100 miles, so now he is older and stronger and hopefully foot and mouth restrictions lifted, up the mileage and speed and aim for our Bronze Thistle, which includes two 20-mile rides in a set time and a 30-mile ride.'

WOOTTON BLACK MAGIC

NFS 4573
Foaled: 1973
Sire: Green Pastures Monarch
Dam: Miss Maytime
Breeder: H. Hayter
Owner: C. Beaurain

'We first spotted Magic at the Brockenhurst Show when he was owned by Roy and Jean Hawkins and taking part in the parade of ponies for sale. We decided to have him on trial, during which time he did his best to put me off, his favourite trick was when he became excited, rearing and launching himself into the air (this proved most amusing on the drifts during later rides). On another occasion whilst trotting over some poles, he tripped over and landed up in a heap; this was a pony whose jumping was to become his favourite event. However, we still bought him, not sure why! He would never stay in a stable without throwing a tantrum, rearing at the door and kicking back. Many a time the block of five wooden stables had to be put back onto the concrete blocks because he had kicked them off. When turned out, he would jump to and fro from different fields. I never knew where to find him. He is terrified of anything bigger than a car, he shakes and his legs give way at the sight of a tractor.

'Many times I have ended up on a sat-down pony in a ditch. We regularly hunted with the New Forest buckhounds, participated in as many events as possible. We soon formed a team winning the first two jumping classes we entered, put us straight into a 3 foot class in our first show, in which we were 2nd. Magic won numerous Mountain & Moorland WHP classes, including the Baker Cup at the Breed Show. He loved show jumping, cross country and in one year he won three championships at Langford Farm. He won the SHS HT for three years, one year completing the whole course in 3 minutes 50 seconds. He also competed in the point-to-point most years, once being 3rd. He has won over 800 rosettes and 50 trophies for every event from showing, gymkhana and long distance rides. His showing could have been better but Magic had the idea that if he loaded to the show, he certainly would not load back, making him very fit looking, hence a bit too sleek for the showing classes. When Magic was about nineteen years old, I decided to semi-retire him as I had another Forest pony.

'One day I noticed he was lame, but was not sure why. Eventually we had him X-rayed and the vet found he had an incredibly infected pedal bone nearly to the joint, not something they had dealt with before, the prognosis was not good and as he was old euthanasia was suggested. However, after much discussion with Mr Gould, he decided to "give it a go". It meant cutting the front off the hoof and scooping out the infected bone. This would mean 18 months to 2 years with sterile bandaging and keeping him stabled. Possibly just to kill the infection enough that he would not have to be put down. He stood bravely on a plastic sheet in the middle of the yard whilst three vets drilled his foot open and cut away the bone. The bandages had to be changed daily and kept totally sterile. He now stabled perfectly. He wore out three equi boots and we now have shares in vetrap. I won't say what all this cost us, but then again what is the price of a friend? Not a speck of dirt was allowed near Magic's foot, which was totally wrapped up all the time. I knew he was recovering when he bolted out of the stable to a friend's field, equi boot and bandage flying. I got him just before the last bandage came off exposing the bone, he was not lame. We took more x-rays, the bone was growing back and, yes, he was sound. Now 23 years old, he has a new rider and is winning more than ever. He won the ridden New Forest at Bashley, the adult WHP at the Breed Show, 9th in the NF ridden at the New Forest and placed in the BSPS WHP classes at Wincanton and Romsey shows. He is also back jumping winning his first jumping class for four years, an open at Langford Farm and the open New Forest at the Breed Show 1995. Magic is much better behaved and loads to and from shows with no bother. He is a real personality and much loved. Who knows what is in store!'

PHOENIX

'I have just made a long journey to Wales to collect a 20-year-old New Forest mare. I bought her for a song at Beaulieu Road 11 years ago, she was packed tight in a pen with other mares all too old or not hardy enough for the Forest and all I could see of her was her head but I was so taken with her lovely eye I got quite excited. As she was not then registered I had no idea of her age. When she came in the ring she was in very poor condition but the frame seemed all right so we bought her. I later discovered her owner had had her in a field all summer prior to the sale in a fruitless attempt to fatten her. All winter we wormed and fed, fed and wormed without any apparent sign of improvement, but in the spring when she shed her very long coat, the improvement began and after a summer on good grass she was round and gleaming and has remained so ever since. We called her Phoenix because we really thought she had risen from the ashes. We tracked down her breeder and the area where she had always run, near the Naked Man, and found she was a grand-daughter of Goodenough and related to Brookside Olivia.

'One of the pleasures of breeding native ponies is the larger-than-life characters that natives seem to attract and Elizabeth and Carl are no exception. Both talented musicians, Elizabeth played with the Halle and was principal violinist with Sadlers Wells for many years, and Carl was an opera singer. Eight years ago they threw their musical careers overboard, bought a small farm in Wales, bought Phoenix and several colts from me to join the ponies they already owned. Their great talent seems to be nursing sick animals and Phoenix is proof of this. Phoenix was struck by lightning and lay paralysed for three weeks, unable to move on a cold Welsh mountain. They built a shelter of straw bales round her, fed, nursed and gave her the will to live, and all this time she was suckling a foal, she is a marvellous milker who puts everything into her foals. After three weeks she managed to stand but had radial paralysis on one side. Gradually she recovered and now all there is to see is a white line down her shoulder where the lightning struck.

'Before going to Wales Phoenix had two colts, one went with her, the other is now licensed and belongs to a vet nearby. Over the years Elizabeth and Carl have told me what good offspring Phoenix had produced, mainly cross-bred, and this year we went to see them. When Phoenix was covered by a 15.2hh TB she produced a 15.2hh offspring with masses of bone, when she went to a 15.0hh Arab, it was again a 15.0hh filly with bone, but what really made me regret having sold her was her two pure New Forest fillies. Again this year Elizabeth and Carl performed another miraculous feat of nursing when Phoenix's foal had what they think could be tetanus, although their vet thought it could be what is known as Black Leg in cattle. The foal was certainly very ill but has now made a complete recovery.

'As Elizabeth and Carl had nine of Phoenix's daughters and grand-daughters they were not going to put her in foal and offered her to me to see if I could be lucky enough to get another foal or two before she retires from breeding, but with the guarantee that this marvellous old mare, who is such a wonderful character, will stay with one or other of us for the rest of her life. '

PRIORY CATKIN II

'It is with great sadness that we have to record the death of our wonderful much loved pony, Priory Catkin II at the age of 21. In a freak accident whilst out in the field she tore the ligaments from her pelvis which resulted in a massive haematoma. She was a real "pony in a million".

'In 1978 when we lived in Oxted, Surrey, I wanted to buy a weanling to bring on and break myself. As I am of a nervous disposition I decided that a New Forest would have the right temperament – willing but tolerant, with the sense to overlook my mistakes. I also wanted a pony that would be up to height.

'I visited several studs including Mrs C. Green's Priory Stud in Berkshire. As soon as I saw Catkin I knew she was the right one as she had such a kind eye. She was by Priory Black Boots out of Tidebrook Hazel. She proved to be the perfect choice. In the 21 years we had her she never kicked or bit anyone, or indeed any other horse. Nor to my knowledge did she ever once refuse a fence. In her whole life we never hit her; "Catkin!" spoken in reproachful tones was quite enough to stop her from doing anything disapproved of.

'She was very easy to break and was always extremely willing to carry out her rider's wishes. She won various mixed native pony classes in hand as a youngster (in Surrey there were no special classes for New Forests). Later under saddle she won Mixed M&M ridden classes and we brought her for the first time to Brockenhurst for the Breed Show in 1983 when she was 5. This was the first time she had competed against other top NF ponies and we were thrilled with her results. I quote from the NFPB&CS report on that show:

'"Another competitor who will hopefully inspire others was Mrs S. Carlyle from Surrey who, with her daughter Lizzy, brought along Priory Catkin II, surely the perfect family pony. Ridden by either mother or daughter, the mare competed tirelessly all day, crowning a string of successes by becoming our qualifier of the NPS Mountain & Moorland Ridden Championship at Olympia."

'Catkin lived out and we had a real job to keep her from growing a thick winter coat before December. At Olympia she was unplaced but in spite of her youth she behaved impeccably, enjoying all the lights and the crowds, the bands and the applause.

'From then on Catkin competed with great success in Dressage, Show Jumping, Cross Country and Horse Trials. She attended all Pony Club activities, including Camp. She represented Limpsfield Riding Club on numerous occasions in their Show Jumping and Dressage teams. She was a brilliant hunter and well known in the Old Surrey & Burstow country for giving a lead to huge Thoroughbreds over any sort of difficult or scary fence. Among her successes she won the

Warlingham Pony Club Open Two Day event against 16hh horses from all over the country.

'When Lizzy left school she trained for some time with Lucy Thompson, member of the Irish three-day-event team, and the then European champion, sponsored by Asprey. At home Catkin gave a lead to Lucy's young horses over fences, and, where eligible (she was too small for official BHS events), she travelled in the Asprey horsebox to compete alongside them.

'Whilst we were moving house Catkin was lent to a friend to teach her young nervous daughter to ride. In a year Charlotte progressed from scratch to hunting and competing at Pony Club level. Catkin gave her such confidence that afterwards she insisted on having a New Forest pony of her own (Willoway Highlight).

'Over the years we brought her regularly to the Breed Show (a 200 mile round trip) where she achieved many successes. After we moved to the Forest she won the Children's Race at the Boxing Day point-to-point (ridden by Rebecca Lees).

'Catkin never needed to be tied up when we were away from home. We used to leave her to graze at will and she never strayed further than 50 yards from us. She did not need to be tied up either for treatment of minor ailments or cuts; she had complete trust in us, as indeed we did in her.

'In 1999 Catkin, at the age of 21 competed in two shows: the NF Pony Enthusiasts in May, where she qualified for the Super Solvitax Ridden Veteran Championship at Malvern (sadly we were unable to make the long journey there), and the Breed Show in August. Here she jointly won the Burley Cup for Dressage and was placed 3rd in a strong Working Pony class over a 3'3" course. She also completed six various jumping rounds all without fault.

'So we feel that Catkin was an outstanding pony – even for a New Forest!'

SILVERLEA ROZENCAVALIER JA
Breeders: Mr & Mrs Stainer
Sire: Silverlea Spotlight
'Rupert to his friends. 138cm Show Jumping Champion Horse of the Year Show 2002.
'Rozencavalier was sold at two years to Mrs Maureen Rayner and presented by her to run on the open forest in 1993 and 1994. Nine progeny were registered. Later he was gelded and his introduction at Broadley Farm to a life under saddle was not an easy one. Alan Ingram

Silverlea Rozencavalier

became his new owner and sold him on to a home on the Sussex / Kent border.

'Tori Barker visited that yard to see another pony, saw Rozencavalier, liked what she saw and bought him! When she started work on him she realised he was used to a saddle but terrified of having someone on that saddle – if you got on, you didn't move a muscle! Tori said you couldn't have a nicer pony to deal with in the stable but it became obvious to her, by virtue of his size, he could only be a child's pony. It meant a lot of quiet work and a great deal of patience. She loose jumped him and was amazed at his ability. The higher the jumps the more he enjoyed it! She decided in that small chestnut body was a very talented pony. After eighteen months of dedication she was confident she had produced a pony capable of taking a brave, competent child to the top. A father and daughter from the North visited with a view to purchase. They agreed he was a good pony but in their opinion he would never be special! He was eventually sold to Belinda Penny. Limes Farm EC report in the *Horse & Hound* referred to Silverlea Rozencavalier, a six-year-old New Forest pony who had a very successful day. His first season affiliated put between £300 and £400 on his card. His life height certificate registered 132 cm so he was quite small to jump in 138 cm competitions, but, as Tori said, he was an outstanding jumper, very fast but accurate. Belinda in due course moved on to 148s and he then passed on to Lucy Pheasant.

'After time he joined the Moore family from Crockstead Park EC and he was partnered by Emma Jane Moore. Practically every week his name appeared in the show jumping results in the *Horse & Hound*. His HOYS ticket was assured when he won at the Bicton Arena. He was a member of the England team who won gold in the Home Pony International and at the 2002 Hickstead Derby Meeting he notched up a win and two seconds.

'No one could deny he had been an outstanding success, but could a 132 cm New Forest Pony win the 138 Championship at the Horse of the Show? Twenty-four top ponies had qualified across the country throughout the year. The day of the final dawned and the International Arena at the NEC Birmingham started at 7.30 am with the 128 cm championship. At 3.15pm on that Saturday afternoon the telephone rang at Silverlea from the NF Pony Promotion Group who had a stand at Birmingham to pass the wonderful news that Silverlea Rozencavalier was the Champion. Emma Jane Moore has now moved onto 148s but Rozencavalier was being watched by his potential new owners and is now in Southern Ireland to be jumped by a twelve-year-old. It is unlikely that much will be heard about him now which is disappointing. One wonders whether the man from the North will have changed his mind about the good pony that would never be special. It really is a rags to riches story and the first ever New Forest pony to win this prestigious title. The BSJA have listed the top ten 138 cm ponies – he takes the sixth spot with winnings in 2002 of £1,277.

'It is difficult to say where the jump comes from in so many of the Silverlea ponies. Slipper and Brookside David seem to be the key. Silverlea Flash Harry and Silverlea Michaelmas were both foals of Silverlea Chocolate Girl, a grand-daughter of Slipper. Silverlea Spotlight is by Silverlea Flash Harry who has a line back to Brookside David. The 2002 French Reserve National Champion Silverlea Simply Red is by Silverlea Flash Harry. Silverlea Mermade II is by Silverlea Spotlight – she jumps internationally in Spain and there are many Grand Prix ponies in France and Belgium born on Stanpit Marsh, the birthplace of Silverlea Rozencavalier on 7th May 1991. On the other hand perhaps there is something in the remark made by Penny Rendle who helps every year when the foals are weaned on the Christchurch marshes "If they can't jump when they leave this place, they never will!"

'May luck be with Rozencavalier and his new rider in his coming years in Ireland.'

Burley Gossip.

BURLEY GOSSIP

Foaled: 1991
Sire: Peveril Peter Piper
Dam: Weirs Aveline
Breeder: Gill Wright
Owner: Mrs R E Launder and ridden by her daughter Charlotte

'Burley Gossip has taken Charlotte from a novice jumping minimus fences to winning the 138 Junior M & M WHP at the BSPS Championships at Peterborough.

'During 2002 she also qualified for UK Riders regional finals Show Jumping, represented the Pony Club Dressage Team, won a Ffrethi Intermediate Ridden, qualifying for the NPS Championships, won Heritage WHP and Shearwater WHP at Wessex County qualifying for BSPS and Ponies (UK) Championships on the same day. She qualified for four classes in all at Ponies (UK) including Style & Performance which she won at Merrist Wood, was also placed in New Forest in-hand at Ponies (UK), South of England Show, was 7th in NF & Conn. Ridden HOYS qualifier where she also jumped clear in HOYS. WHP placed 8th in HOYS WHP at New Forest Show with another clear round and 6th in the M & M WHP at Royal Windsor Horse Show.

'Gossip has also just reintroduced Charlotte to cross country after a bad accident with a previous pony.

'As well as being a brilliant and versatile competition pony, Gossip travels well and always settles into strange stables without bother. At home she is an affectionate pony, easy to catch, well mannered in stable, good to shoe and with vet, traffic proof and hacks out alone or in any company. Charlotte has never fallen off her and as far as I know no-one ever has.

'As Charlotte's legs get longer and mum gets older we may break her to harness, which I am sure she will take to as well as everything else she has done.

'It would be difficult to find a more perfect pony.'

Gossip and Beacon Pieris are so far the only ponies to achieve grade 3 jumping.

MERRIE MISS TIDY

Foaled: 1992
Sire: Merrie Marmalade
Dam: Merrie Mistella
Owner: Margaret Fogg

'Merrie Miss Tidy won two trophies for highest points over the 3 days of the Red Dragon ride in Wales 2003, covering 50 kilometres each day in Graded Rides.

'In the three years I have owned "Misty" we have covered some 1,571 kilometres in competitions, backed up by countless distances in training and getting fit!

'Misty won the Endurance Great Britain (EGB) South East Group Novice Trophy in her first season of competition, and the EGB South East Group Best Native Award in her second year. She is a great ambassador for her breed in a sport where most people think that you cannot really compete without an Arab horse to ride.'

Margaret Fogg

SABINA'S SILVER SHADOWS

NFM 2002
Foaled: 1997
Sire: Peveril Peterborough
Dam: Silverlea Halina

'Known as Petal. Silver Shadows was ridden champion at The New Forest Breed Show in August 2002, her rider was Ehsan Roudiana who qualified the mare for the Bailey's Horse Feeds Mountain and Moorland Ridden Championship, held at the Olympia Christmas Show.

'After several months of build-up, with lungeing and strapping, the day started for real on Sunday morning when, after a morning hack, she had her bath. Plenty of warm water and shampoo, and she finally started looking white rather than khaki! We left for London on Sunday afternoon, and arrived after an uneventful journey. I was expecting her to be unsettled in her temporary stable, but she settled in and started eating as if she did it every day.

'On Monday morning, the native ponies were allocated an hour and a half to warm up in the main arena before the crowds arrive – from 7 to 9.30 am. This meant a very early start as Petal had to have finished her breakfast by 6 am. It was very close to chaos – ponies everywhere! But again, she coped really well and we were almost looking forward to the big event! Beautifully ridden by her owner, Fiona Biddle, she went very nicely in her individual show and won the Best of Breed award. Overall, we were very pleased with her performance and not being placed didn't detract from the day at all – she was a credit to her father and to us. After the end presentation she went back to the stable for a well earned rest while Fiona, Jodie and I went to put some pressure on our credit cards! The next day she went back out with her friends and was soon a lovely shade of brown again!

'We're already planning our campaign for next year, and aiming high!'

MATLEY DARK LIGHTNING

'A friend of mine was so taken with my New Forest ponies she asked me to look for one for her. She wanted a filly that she could show and later breed from. At Devizes last May there was a sale of ponies, mostly New Forest yearlings. They were all very wild, rushing about in converted barns. It was difficult to see them, but I did my best and picked one out for her, a dark bay with a white star, plus three others for another friend. We took all four ponies back to my friend's place, she has a barn with four stables in it. We drove the four ponies out of the horse box and into the stables, two ponies in each, where we gave them hay and water and left them for the night. The next morning bright and early we set out with head collars in one hand and wormers in the other. Two of the fillies we found fairly quiet and soon, with a bit of coaxing, we had them haltered and wormed. The last two proved to be nowhere near as easy, and would not respond to coaxing. Both ponies were very frightened and certainly did not like humans. After several hours and much fighting, we got our way. The next few weeks they were left to get used to their new home, but they remained nearly as wild. One day, the Annual Breed Show schedule came through the post and my friend was keen to take her new filly. I said, "You can't be serious, we only have 5 weeks and they are still very wild, we can't catch them, let alone lead them, their feet have to be trimmed, they have to be groomed, loaded into a horse box and tied up as well as being able to be with strange people, impossible." She was serious! So we moved her filly and one of the quieter ones down the lane to my stables where I could spend more time with them individually.

'The first thing we did was to register them, Matley Dark Lightning because she had a mark on her side like a streak of lightning. The other filly we called Fir Tree Crescent Moon because she had a mark like a crescent moon on her face. The day before the show they had their tails and socks washed. Both fillies were entered in Yearling Filly that was born on the Forest and in Yearling filly stud section. The first class was Forest bred, the Judge pulled in her winner and to my amazement we were pulled in second with Crescent Moon coming in 5th. The next class was the stud section and again we were pulled in second, two prizes in one day, not bad for a pony that five weeks before was as wild as a hawk. The second place in the Stud bred class made us eligible for the Forest Bred Championship as the first placed had gone to a stud bred pony. The championship came, we were up against the highest placed ponies in all other stud bred classes, my friend watched with bated breath and when we were pulled in eighth she left as she was due to do her first ever class, showing my thirty-year-old pony in the veterans. We all did our individual shows and the judge pulled in the pony of her choice as Champion, then walking down the line she pulled us forward. Dark Lightning was Reserve Champion and I was delighted. With tears in my eyes we did our lap of honour and went to find the Veteran ring and my friend who also was very happy with a first in the Veterans. What a successful day, a fifth, a first, two seconds and a Reserve Champion. My friend was delighted and now can't wait for the summer and all the shows!'

Jenny Guscott

RODLEASE GREY DAWN'S 'GLEN JEFFERYS'

'This is the best way for us to describe ourselves. As every New Forest pony owner knows – they're in charge. I could write pages and pages about a personality such as "Dawnie" especially as she has completely changed my life, but space is limited. When she first came to me three years ago she looked like Mrs Blobby. For this reason her then owners wanted me to help her lose weight. The fact that I had recently had to have my spotted gelding put down, and had nothing to ride made me think this was a good idea. I didn't realise then how much I would love her. It wasn't long before I felt I didn't ever want to part with her but I knew her owner didn't want to sell her. We started going to shows, doing a little dressage and having wonderful results. She started losing weight and beginning to look more wonderful all the time. But I knew the day would come when she would have to go back. When Christmas arrived, I will never forget it. I was given a large envelope from my husband, Steve. When I opened it, I found Dawn's registration certificate – she belonged to me. I was absolutely thrilled.

'Dawn has also made it possible for me to achieve a life-time ambition – perhaps I should say Dawn and Valerie Millwood – to compete side-saddle. We had a lovely time at Malvern Side-saddle Championships last year: 2nd in Teams Dressage, 8th small riding horse, 5th Restricted turnout and 5th mixed M & M. This season she has already won 1st time out, in Novice Adult Equitation. What a star! I would also like to say that Dawn has also made it possible for me to meet so many marvellous people who have known for a lot longer than I have, how wonderful the New Forest pony is – especially Avril Darnton, who bred "Dawnie" out of Boundway Stable and Bunny McGrath, the owner and breeder of her sire Vernons Vespers. I can't imagine a time when I would be without a New Forest pony. Thank you Dawn.'

MERRIE MILLET ('BIRD')

'Takes to the stage in the ballet Giselle.

'I did not think we would have the opportunity to see Giselle, but special arrangements were made, and we were invited to watch the Saturday night performance from the wings. Bird had proved to be quite happy with an audience, his only response to applause being to look even prouder – and he knew his part, even to his musical cue!

'It was a good job I had not seen the lift till then as it was a commercial type, open, and as we descended we could look down onto the stage. His ears pricked, Bird calmly looked down at dancers warming up. Once at stage level, he totally "switched off", patiently dozing, although any dancers in his vicinity were regarded with interest.

'As the first act started he was tacked up; he had his own saddle cloth made to match the ballerina's dress. Although he was to be ridden side saddle, an ordinary saddle was used to enable the ballerina to slide off easily. Whilst we waited he was visited by a steady stream of dancers, who made a fuss of him before they went on stage. A small step was used to mount the ballerina - on the 'wrong' side! She also sat and slid down on the offside. Her costume was long, and covered Bird's back to below his hocks, they had had to shorten it after the dress rehearsal, for it dropped to the floor and threatened to drag her off. We were told he had learnt his musical cue very quickly, and indeed when the music changed and the horns blew Bird marched forward to enter, at rear centre stage. A walk around the limited area of the front stage, then he stood centre back as the ballerina slid off to join the action – ears pricked, he waited patiently for his exit, then left the stage with the rest of the hunting party.

'But his test was not ended there, he had to wait off stage until the interval, when the lift could be operated to return Bird to street level. He did all this with no "accidents" of the personal nature on stage. (This could have been messy as well as embarrassing)

The production has now gone on tour, but this was the only theatre that could take Bird, so his excursion into drama is now over – for this year. But it is possible that when the production is repeated in 2000 that he may be asked to return.

'From this narrative, you might think that Bird is a quiet, sensible pony. No, he never bucks or rears, but he is not a novice ride, being of a nervous and excitable nature. We always try to allow time at shows, before classes, so he can settle, and then he does his job well. To tell the truth we did not think he would last beyond rehearsals. Given his temperament, it makes what he did even more amazing (no calming agents of any sort were used).

'On returning home, Bird continued with his normal work, unaffiliated dressage and showing. Now the winter PUK qualifiers, and rapidly qualified for the championships, picking up his first ridden qualifier, two weeks later winning his first ridden championship.

PYLEWELL GIRL FRIDAY

13.1 hh owned by Jonathan Stewart aged 13 and her activities during the 1992 school holidays seem worthy of comment. At Christmas they were hunting in the Forest and then early in the Easter holidays were off on a Pony Club Polo Course, soon after she played in two area polo matches including one at the Royal Berkshire Club. Then the great Event, a three-day visit to Jonathan's uncle, to Exmoor and two days hunting for 'Friday' with the Devon & Somerset Staghounds, as a Forest pony she caused much comment. Next the Summer holidays and seven Pony Club Polo Tournaments, including Epsom, Kirtlington, Cirencester, Tidworth and Windsor culminating in qualifying for the championships at Cowdray Park, where the team came fifth. In between these tournaments they did general riding and Pony Club activities, including Tethrathlon, though hunting and polo are what the pair enjoy most. The Family also own Silverlea JackFlash, on the right in the photograph, ridden by Georgina Stewart. He raced in the Point to Point and finished 2nd as a five year-old. He carries all the members of the family and is used to give a lead to the National Hunt horses, as well as Pony Club activities.

RALPH HAYWARD was a well known New Forest Commoner and breeder of Rowdown New Forest ponies. The following is an article by Ralph lifted from the Annual Report of 1990 which gives an interesting insight into the past.

"Two ponies called Zephyr

'Winning the Veterans' Race with Zephyr on Boxing Day at Wilverley this year brought back memories of another win 42 years ago on practically the same finish at Wilverley, when I won my first New Forest point-to-point, this time on a New Forest pony also called Zephyr. It was the Small Commoners' race for Forest ponies. I believe, at that time, there were only three races, Small Commoners, the Open New Forest ponies and Children's races. We met at Balmer Lawn and the start was from Black Knoll close to New Park and was up hill all the way. As far as I remember, there was quite a good entry in our race. In second place that year was a New Forest gelding called 'Jobey,' owned by Mr George Parker from East Boldre and ridden by Mr Fred Kitcher of Furzey Lodge, uncle to our Senior Agister Brian Ingram. As both ponies travelled in the same lorry and were from the same area, you can imagine that there was quite a celebration that day at Freddies, the local pub at East Boldre, then called the New Inn now the Turf Cutters, but I think that is another story, the less said the better. Suffice to say, a good time was had by all!

'Although the present Zephyr (Mark II) is quite a pony and all character, I believe and hope she still has a lot to show, but it is the first Zephyr (Mark I) I think is worth a mention as she was truly a Forester, to emphasise the virtues and versatility of the New Forest pony.

'I bought Zephyr from Mr Arth Read (senior) of North Gate, Beaulieu, at two-and-a-half years old. She was bay with black points, similar in fact to the present Zephyr. She attained the maximum height of 13.2

and after the normal period of bickering, she was bought for £9, but as I worked for the family farm and butcher's business for which I was given 10/- (50p) a week, I had to talk my mother into lending me the money before I could clinch the deal, but clinched it was and it was a proud 15-year-old that walked up Beaulieu High Street leading that pony and what a topper she turned out to be. I broke her in at three years old and later to harness. Mr Read told me her mother used to trot round to Southampton with a cart loaded with produce to sell two or three times a week.

'Out colt-hunting she was a joy to ride, could stay all day and never tired, with a lively turn of speed that could turn most colts and was sure-footed as a mountain goat. There were no horse trailers at that time so we rode there and rode back, oft times with colts tied either side. At that time, haymaking was becoming mechanised with horse drawn turners and side rakes. Zephyr was able at all these jobs, dung cart, chain harrowing, trace horse turning, raking and when needed, would pull in loads of hay to the rick. In fact there was nothing that pony could not do.

'Another of her jobs was to collect animals from farms and cottages with a float to take into the slaughterhouse at Beaulieu; she always stood not tied and never moved even when a pig was carried up the garden path to the cart and you know how they can protest.

'But, of course, it was not all work, we spent many happy hours riding the Forest. There were Pony Races at Burley and Langley as well as colt-hunting which she seemed to enjoy as much as myself. Remarkably, I can never remember her either lame or sick.

'The Langley Races became fairly regular for a few years until the War; at one race meeting at Langley, to whet the appetite of the public, a challenge race was arranged between Buffy Mansbridge's pony Muss and Ralph Hayward's Zephyr: £5 to the winner, distance two miles. Muss's jockey was Miss P. Mansbridge. Zephyr won that race, which reminds me I never did get the £5.

'Another small episode that emphasises the qualities of a New Forest Pony to be a safe and sensible mount for hunting, Forest work or almost anything, to see danger and get out of trouble happened at one of the Society's own Breed Shows at Burley, at the time when Pony races were still held on Show day; some older members may remember it. The mile race was run on the perimeter of the park outside the show rings and the finish was on the flat in front of the big house. Ropes were tied across the course, I presume to stop the young bloods practising, these were removed, of course, at race time. The rope had somehow been missed and was still in position. I happened to be leading on Zephyr at that point and did not see the rope and neither did anyone else, the first indication that anything was amiss was when Zephyr suddenly rose up and over, she had seen the rope and hopped over it but there was quite a tangle of ponies and riders, luckily no one was hurt, but I think another good example of how a good Forest pony can get you out of trouble.

'At the outbreak of war, my life, like most people's, changed and for the next six and a half years I was away in the Forces. Zephyr once more stepped into the breach for the family: when petrol became short, she was called up to help in the business and spent the war years delivering meat and fish in the butcher's cart and I am told a smart job she made of it.

'I must tell you just one more episode of Zephyr's life as a butcher's rounds pony, one that proved she never forgot her racing days or the trick of sticking to the ropes on corners. We had a lifelong friend and helper in the business who became one of the finest slaughtermen and master butchers you could wish to find; his name was Reg (Whippet) West; his nickname came from the way he whipped in and out of houses on his rounds and he was always smartly turned out. I believe Zephyr in that butcher's cart and Whippet were made for each other, because she could step out and really move that cart.

'This is how the story goes. They were on their way home to the shop after delivering at Exbury, Purlieu and Hill Top. On reaching the Mill at Beaulieu Whippet thought, like the good showman he was, he would show them what a good turnout Hayward's delivery outfit was by flying up the High Street at full trot; however he forgot Zephyr's' racing past, and she must have forgotten she had a cart behind as she shaved the corner the cart, hit the high kerb, turned over and Zephyr arrived at the shop with harness and shafts whilst Whippet and the cart were still down at the bottom of the street. Luckily no one was hurt, except pride!

'This has been just a small peep into the life of Zephyr (Mark 1), the New Forester. As you can gather, it once again proves the New Forest Pony is second to none, when it comes to value and an honest common sense working pony that can be relied on in any situation.

'I rode Zephyr several times again after the war, but she was then getting to be an old lady. The only regret is that her life was so busy she had no time to produce a foal, that's another one we can chalk up to Hitler.'

KNIGHTWOOD WITCH-HUNT

Breeder: Mr P.A. Harvey Richards
Wessex Regional Endurance GB Championship 2004
'After competing in one endurance ride at the end of the 2003 season, I realised my 14.1hh pony had a flare for distance riding. I therefore decided at the beginning of 2004 to really test her abilities, and in order to do this, I decided we would both follow the fast track progression route (to do this she had to be 6 years old or over). This meant that we could quickly progress from Novice level, through Intermediate and up to Advanced level, all in one season. In order to achieve this, we successfully completed all 7 competitive rides that we entered, the total distance of which is 413 km. The final ride of the season was our first one-day 80km graded ride, held on the New Forest.

'The awards we have received for these achievements are as follows: all the rides we entered were graded rides and we accomplished three grade 1s, two grade 2s, one grade 3 and one grade 4. For progressing to Intermediate we received a bronze medal. For progressing to Advanced we received a silver medal. For completing our first one-day 80 km ride we received a distance medal! For riding a total distance of 400 km we will receive a distance medal. We have a total of 1,246 points for the season which has meant we were 2nd place to the 'Pitchford' Trophy at the National awards evening. This is awarded to the registered British native pony achieving most points in any competitive ride throughout the season. At the Wessex regional awards evening we were placed 1st to the 'What Now' Trophy for the highest placed registered British Native pony in the Wessex region. Finally, we were also awarded the 'Myebon' Trophy for being the Wessex regional champions by gaining the most points competing in Wessex run endurance rides. This trophy was accompanied by the Marlpit Trophy, awarded to my Crew for their incredibly hard work throughout the season.

'Without the dedication of my Crew (Tina Elliott, Rhian Williams, Glen Henbest and my parents), all of whom had a very steep learning curve and the support of my husband, who ensured my 4x4 and trailer were in tip-top condition each weekend, I could not have achieved any of this, so I am incredibly grateful to them all.'
Jackie Henbest

To reach the very top in any discipline a pony not only has to have the right pedigree and a good mother to nurture it, but the correct rearing, handling and training, an owner who can afford to compete it and has the patience to give it time, since most ponies are not at their best till they are about eight; and most importantly the right rider. There are dozens of foals every year that never reach their potential because there are not enough good trainers and riders. Not all can be top winners but they should all be capable of doing a good job comfortably. The much loved and successful ponies in this chapter were lucky enough to meet the right people at the right time. Spare a thought for the others, how can we increase the number of people who can rear, train and ride them and so lessen the element of luck?

CONCLUSION

New Forest ponies have proved themselves essential to the survival of the traditional character of the New Forest. They have the adaptability, temperament, athleticism, conformation and movement to compete successfully in any discipline and the strength and stamina to be real family ponies for all aged riders. However, as most are bred in and around the Forest, they are very vulnerable to the possible introduction of new diseases and with a very small percentage of stallions and the inability to totally separate herds for several generations, there is a grave danger of gene loss. So the present stallion scheme is not, in the long term, sustainable; it is time to tackle the mares. This is where the mare grading should help. Hopefully foals advertised by graded mares will be worth more and some breeders will get to know the standard required. Let us all ensure these marvellous ponies continue to give pleasure to many and maintain their traditional habitat. They are an important part of our national heritage.

GLOSSARY

Catch weight – whatever the rider and saddle weigh: no upper or lower limit

Depastured ponies – are turned out on the open Forest to run wild by their owners, who enjoy common of pasture over the Forest. These people are called **Commoners**

Forest trucks were small flat carts often pulled by tugs to the shaft as in wagons rather than by traces

Haunting the area of the Forest in which the pony runs; of variable size to contain food, water and shelter year long usually about one square mile.

M & M Mountain and Moorland: ponies of one of the nine breeds native to the British Isles and tracing to mares who ran for at least three generations on their native mountain, moor or common. This is the definition used in the 1912 Royal Commission and accounts for the inclusion of the Irish Connemara. Recently the Rare Breeds have included the Eriskay, but is this really a breed or merely a herd of Highlands isolated for a long time from the rest of the breed?

ODE – one day event, a competition with dressage, cross-country and show jumping

RDA – Riding for the Disabled

Round bone - the opposite of deirable flat bone, where the joints and sinews are very sharply defined, joints appear rather large and the knees are flat, and shield shaped, viewed from the front. Round bones are rather ill defined and appear round

Tail marked - each Agister cuts a piece out of the pony 's tail, one cuts one slice from the left,one from the right, one cuts two from the left, one two from the right, and one from each side. This shows from which Agister's area the owner comes and that he has paid his annual marking fee for that pony. The mark takes a year to grow out.

WHP – Working hunter pony class, a competition with a round of 'natural', i.e. unpainted jumps with a score for style and an individual ridden show and run out scored for way of going, type, conformation and manners.

INDEX

page references in bold indicate photographs